POCKETS

BUTTERFLIES & MOTHS

Swallowtail butterfly caterpillar

Postman butterfly

Owl butterfly feeding

POCKETS

BUTTERFLIES & MOTHS

Written by
BARBARA TAYLOR

ZEBRA BUTTERFLY

CINNABAR MOTH LAYING EGGS

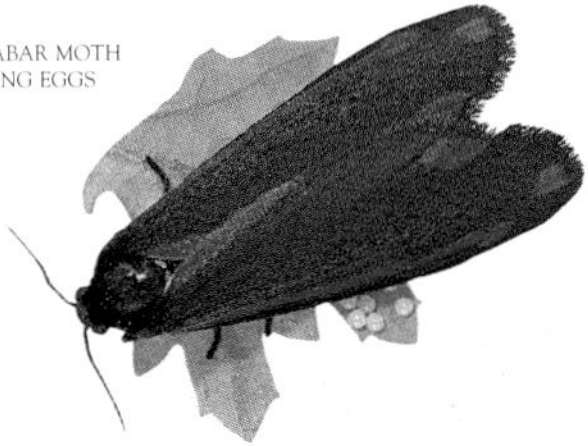

CHRYSALIS OF QUEEN BUTTERFLY

DK

LONDON, NEW YORK,
MUNICH, MELBOURNE, and DELHI

Project editor Caroline Brooke
Art editor Alexandra Brown
Senior editor Hazel Egerton
Senior art editor Jacquie Gulliver
Editorial consultants David Carter, Paul Whalley
Production Josie Alabaster
US editor Constance M. Robinson
US consultant Eric Quinter, Department of Entomology,
American Museum of Natural History

REVISED EDITION
Project editor Sadie Smith
Managing editor Linda Esposito
Managing art editor Jane Thomas
DTP designer Siu Yin Ho
Consultant George Beccaloni
Production Erica Rosen

First American Edition, 1996
Second American Edition, 2004
Published in the United States by
DK Publishing, Inc., 375 Hudson Street,
New York, New York 10014

04 05 06 07 08 10 9 8 7 6 5 4 3 2

A catalog record for this book is available from the Library of Congress.

ISBN 0-7566-0204-1
Color reproduction by Colourscan, Singapore
Printed and bound in Italy by L.E.G.O.

Discover more at
www.dk.com

Contents

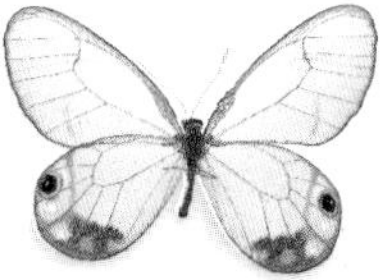

HOW TO USE THIS BOOK

These pages show you how to use *Pockets: Butterflies & Moths*. The book is divided into sections, each opening with a picture page. There is an introductory section at the beginning of the book and a reference section at the back. The central six sections look at butterflies and moths in different habitats.

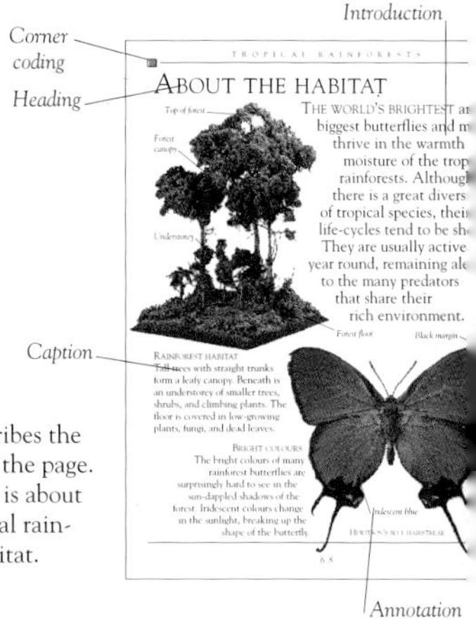

HABITATS

The main section of the book is arranged into habitats. In each habitat section you will find information on the habitat, and examples of the types of moths and butterflies that live there.

CORNER CODING

Corners of the habitat pages are color-coded to remind you which habitat section you are in.

- TEMPERATE WOODLANDS
- TROPICAL RAIN FORESTS
- WETLANDS
- GRASSLANDS AND BARRENS
- DRY REGIONS AND CAVES
- ARCTIC AND MOUNTAINS

HEADING

This describes the subject of the page. This page is about the tropical rain-forest habitat.

INTRODUCTION

This provides a clear, general overview of the subject. After reading the introduction, you should have an idea of what the pages are about.

CAPTIONS AND ANNOTATIONS

Each illustration has a caption. Annotations, in *italics*, point out features of an illustration and usually have leader lines.

Running heads

These remind you which section you are in. The left-hand page gives the section name. The right-hand page gives the subject. This "About the Habitat" page is in the Tropical Rain Forests section.

Fact boxes

Many pages have fact boxes. These contain at-a-glance information about the subject. This fact box gives details such as the area of rain forest that is cut down every second.

Reference section

This section has yellow pages and appears at the back of the book. You will find useful facts, figures, and charts. These pages show which habitats and species are at risk.

Running head *Fact box*

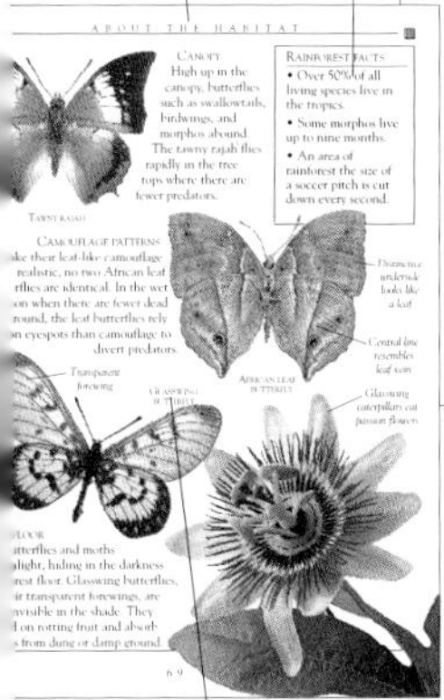

Label

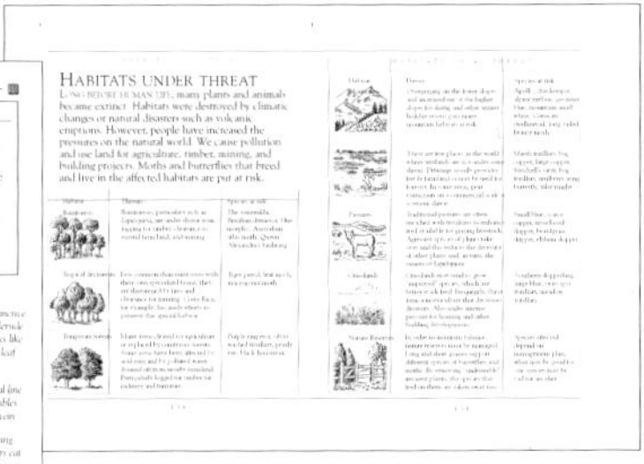

Glossary

At the back of the book is a glossary that explains the more complicated or technical words that appear in the text.

Labels

For extra clarity, some pictures are accompanied by labels. These may provide extra information, or identify a picture when it is not immediately obvious from the text what it is.

Index

There are two indexes at the back of the book. The subject index lists every subject alphabetically. The common and scientific name index lists all the moths and butterflies that are in the book.

INTRODUCTION TO BUTTERFLIES AND MOTHS

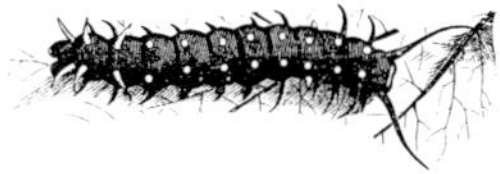

BUTTERFLIES AND MOTHS

FOSSIL OF MOTH'S WING

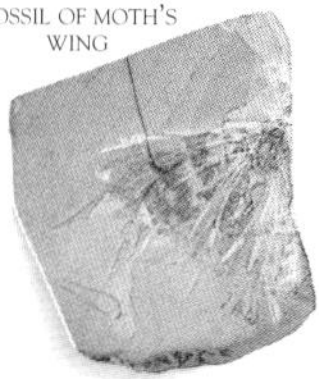

FROM BRILLIANT blue Morpho butterflies to giant Atlas moths, these insects have an amazing variety of shapes, sizes, and colors. They can be distinguished from other insects by their long, hollow feeding tube (proboscis) and by the dustlike scales covering their wings and bodies.

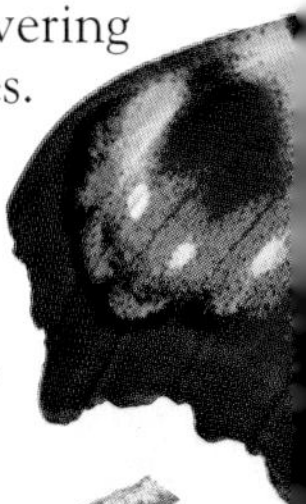

DINOSAUR DAYS

Moths first appeared on Earth between 100 and 190 million years ago during the age of the dinosaurs. Butterflies came on the scene much later – about 40 million years ago. They probably evolved alongside flowering plants.

CLOSE-UP OF WING

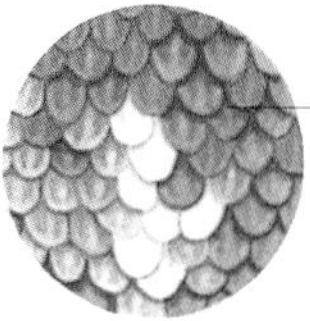

LEPIDOPTERA FACTS

- Butterflies and moths belong to the insect order Lepidoptera, meaning "scaly wings."
- There are about 170,000 known species of Lepidoptera. Only 10 percent are butterflies; the rest are moths.
- There may be 200 to 600 scales per square millimeter of wing.

LIFE CYCLE

Each butterfly or moth goes through four distinct stages during its life. It starts as an egg that hatches into a caterpillar. The caterpillar eventually changes into a pupa, from which the adult emerges.

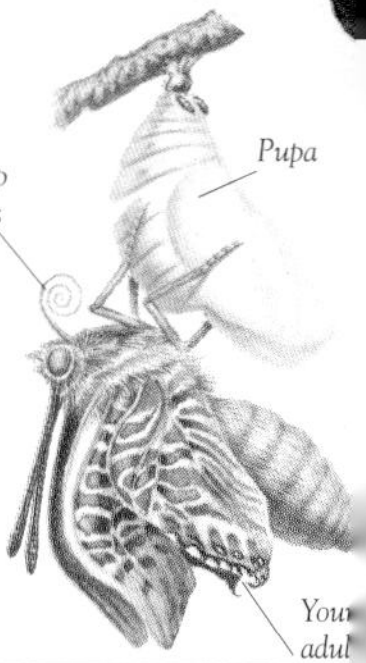

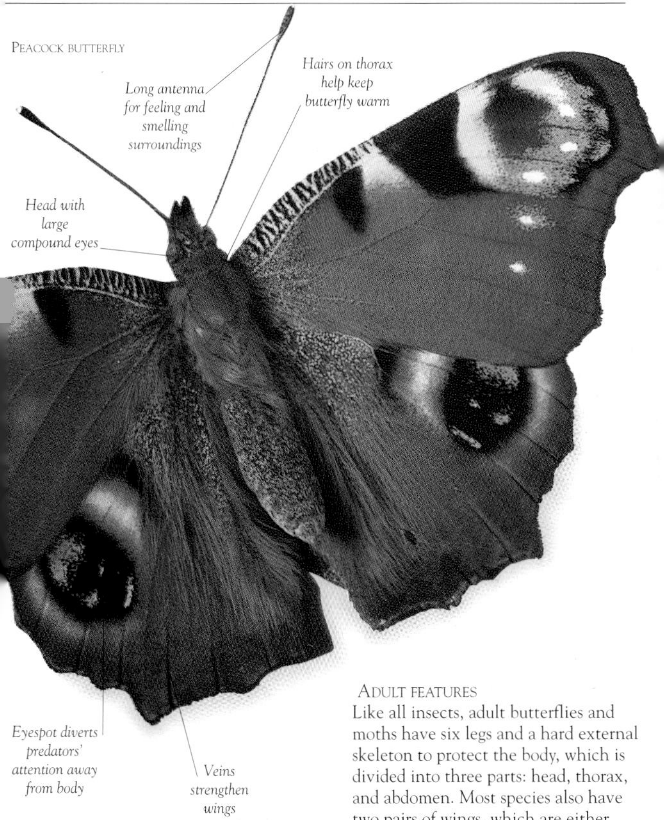

ADULT FEATURES

Like all insects, adult butterflies and moths have six legs and a hard external skeleton to protect the body, which is divided into three parts: head, thorax, and abdomen. Most species also have two pairs of wings, which are either hooked or held together in flight.

Telling the difference

The division of Lepidoptera into butterflies and moths is an artificial one, based on a number of observable differences. Most butterflies fly by day and are brightly colored. Moths tend to be night fliers and have drab-colored wings, although some do fly by day and have bright colors. When resting, butterflies usually hold their wings upright, while moths spread out their wings or fold them flat over their bodies.

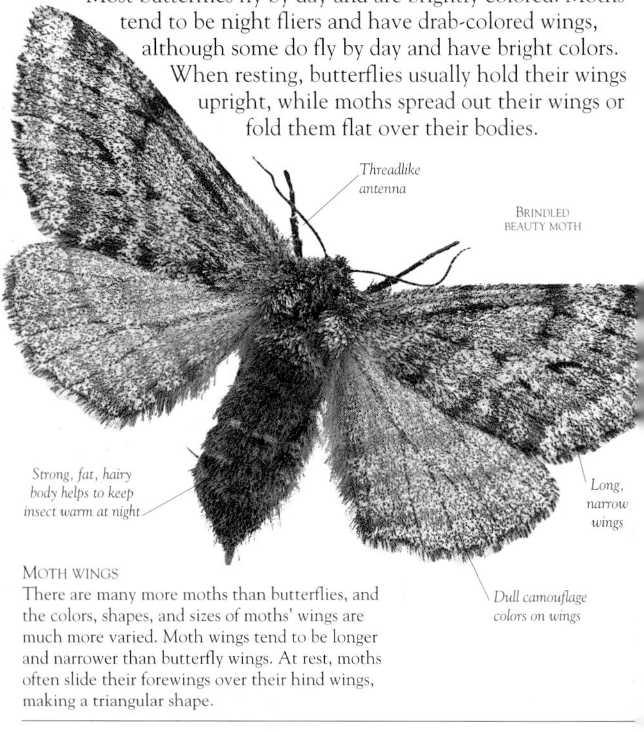

BRINDLED BEAUTY MOTH

MOTH WINGS
There are many more moths than butterflies, and the colors, shapes, and sizes of moths' wings are much more varied. Moth wings tend to be longer and narrower than butterfly wings. At rest, moths often slide their forewings over their hind wings, making a triangular shape.

Butterfly wings

When butterflies land to feed or rest, they are vulnerable to attack from predators. A typical butterfly shows only the undersides of its wings when it rests. The undersides tend to be patterned to camouflage the resting butterfly.

Antennae

A good way to tell the difference between a butterfly and a moth is to look at the antennae. A butterfly antenna has a club on the end; moths have various types of antennae, ranging from single strands to feathery branches.

Butterfly or moth?

Hedylid "moths" from South America are hard to categorize. They are probably more closely related to butterflies than to moths. Although they have mothlike antennae, their bodies and their caterpillars are like those of butterflies.

TYPES OF MOTHS

THERE IS AN incredible variety in the size, color, and shape of moths, from the spectacular Emperor moths and bright Burnets to the small Micromoths and dull-colored Owlet moths. They are grouped into over 100 families. These pages show just five examples of the many families.

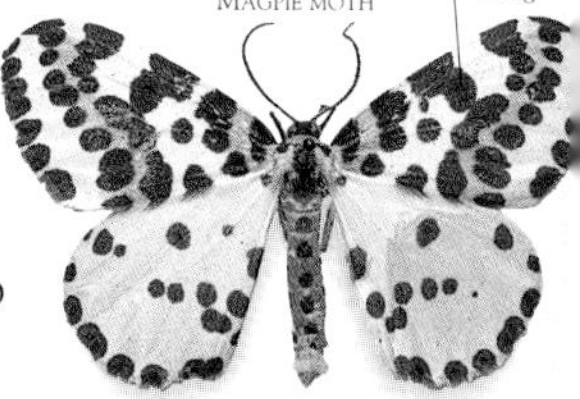

MAGPIE MOTH

GEOMETRIDAE
Geometers have thin bodies, large rounded wings, and a weak, fluttering flight. In some species, the females are wingless. The caterpillars "loop" across their food plants, as if measuring them.

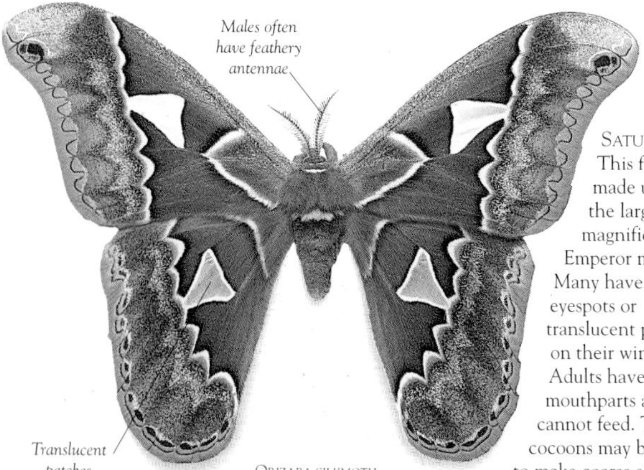

ORIZABA SILKMOTH

SATURNIIDAE
This family is made up of the large and magnificent Emperor moths. Many have eyespots or translucent patches on their wings. Adults have no mouthparts and so cannot feed. Their cocoons may be used to make coarse silk.

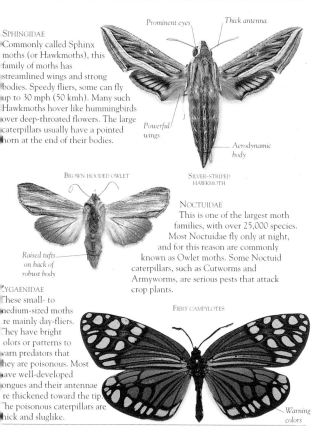

SPHINGIDAE
Commonly called Sphinx moths (or Hawkmoths), this family of moths has streamlined wings and strong bodies. Speedy fliers, some can fly up to 30 mph (50 kmh). Many such Hawkmoths hover like hummingbirds over deep-throated flowers. The large caterpillars usually have a pointed horn at the end of their bodies.

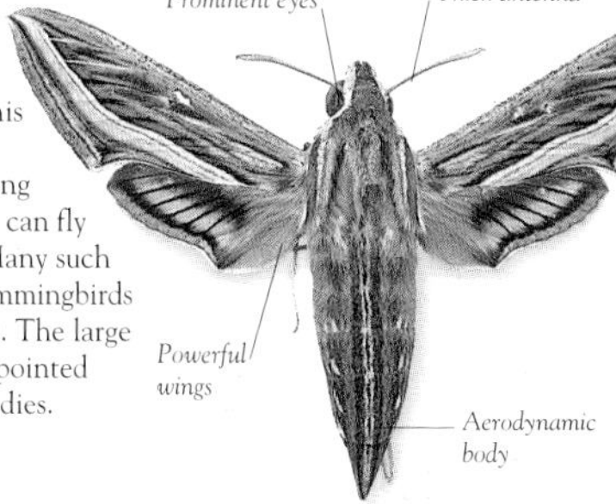

SILVER-STRIPED HAWKMOTH

BROWN HOODED OWLET

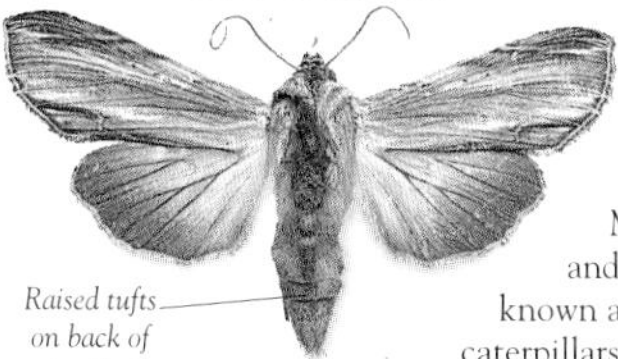

NOCTUIDAE
This is one of the largest moth families, with over 25,000 species. Most Noctuidae fly only at night, and for this reason are commonly known as Owlet moths. Some Noctuid caterpillars, such as Cutworms and Armyworms, are serious pests that attack crop plants.

:YGAENIDAE
Γhese small- to nedium-sized moths re mainly day-fliers. Γhey have bright olors or patterns to varn predators that hey are poisonous. Most ave well-developed ongues and their antennae re thickened toward the tip. Γhe poisonous caterpillars are hick and sluglike.

FIERY CAMPYLOTES

TYPES OF BUTTERFLIES

ALTHOUGH BUTTERFLIES are remarkable for their bold and brilliant colors and beautiful shapes, there are fewer species of butterflies than there are species of moths. Butterflies are usually grouped into five families.

Large, robust body and head

BRAZILIAN SKIPPER

HESPERIIDAE
The butterflies of this family are commonly known as Skippers. Unlike other butterflies, they frequently lack clubbed antennae and, when resting, they fold their forewings over their backs.

Iridescent colors flash in sunlight
Eyespots and tails create a false head to confuse predators

PAPILIO PALINURUS SWALLOWTAIL

PAPILIONIDAE
These large, colorful butterflies tend be powerful fliers. Many have "tails" their hind wings and are popularly known as Swallowtails. This family includes the tailless Birdwings, fou in tropical Australasia.

PIERIDAE

These butterflies are mostly white, yellow, or orange. Their bright colors come from waste products, which are deposited inside their scales. Though many species are tropical, they are found in all regions of the world and many migrate.

CABBAGE BUTTERFLY

Simple black wing markings

Body covered in hairlike white scales

SILVER-STUDDED BLUE

LYCAENIDAE

About 40 percent of all butterflies belong to this family of small, jewel-like butterflies. It includes the Blues, Coppers, and Hairstreaks. Males and females are often different colors, and the upperside of the wing is a brighter color than the underside.

NYMPHALIDAE

The distinguishing feature of this group is that the two front legs are small and cannot be used for walking. The family includes some of the most brilliant butterflies in the world, such as the Emperors, Monarchs, and Fritillaries. They are sometimes called "Brush-footed butterflies" after the thick tufts of scales on the front legs of the males.

White spots on forewing

Scalloped hind wing

PAINTED LADY

WINGS AND FLIGHT

MOTHS AND BUTTERFLIES FLY to escape predators, seek mates, and find food and places to live. Their wings are made of a thin, tough, transparent membrane supported by rigid veins. Flight patterns vary from the energetic darting of Skippers to the fluttering of Cabbage butterflies.

WING VEINS
Butterfly and moth wings have veins that contain air tubes and nerves, and also carry blood. The veins allow the delicate wings to twist, bend, and resist air pressure in flight. The pattern of veins differs from species to species.

JOINING THE WINGS
In butterflies and a few moths, a lobe on the hind wing overlaps and grips the forewing. Most moths have one or more bristles on the hind wing. These fit on the forewing behind a flap or catch.

COMMON BLUE BUTTERFLY

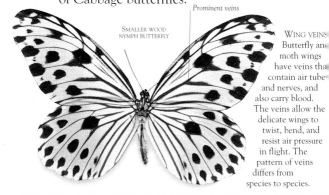

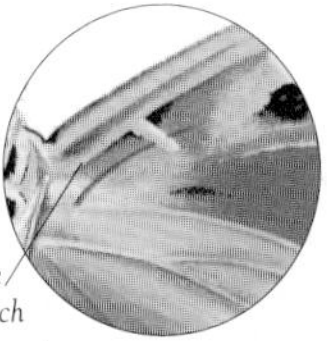

JERSEY TIGER MOTH

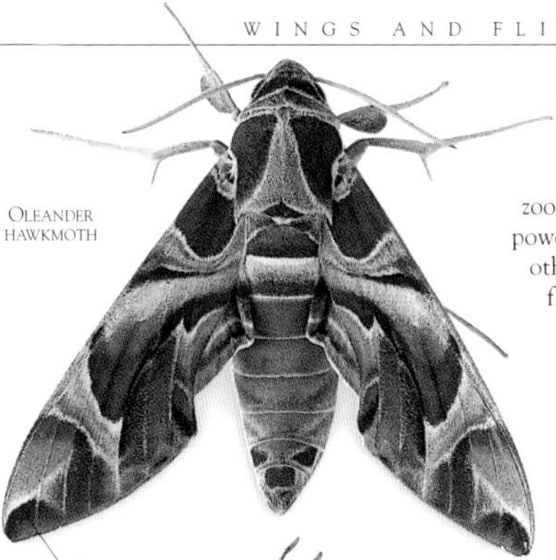

OLEANDER HAWKMOTH

Long, narrow forewing

FAST FLIERS

Resembling tiny jet planes when at rest, Hawkmoths zoom through the dusk on their powerful streamlined wings. Like other night-flying moths, they fly toward the lights of streets and houses, confused by their brightness. They are frequently found on or close to store windows.

Downward flap

SILVER-WASHED FRITILLARY

Gliding on a current of air

Wings move backward and downward, pushing butterfly forward

BUTTERFLY FLIGHT

Most butterflies have a rather lazy "flap and glide" flight. Some butterflies, such as large-winged Swallowtails, are good gliders while others, such as these Fritillaries, can only glide short distances.

MOTHS WITHOUT WINGS

Some female moths, such as this Winter moth, have no wings (or only tiny wings) and cannot fly. By not using their energy for flight, they can instead use it to produce more eggs, which accounts for their huge egg-filled bodies.

Color and scales

Wings are colored and patterned to help moths and butterflies blend with their surroundings, regulate their body temperature, drive away predators, and attract mates. The colors are formed either by pigments contained in the wing scales or by the way the structure of the scales reflects the sunlight. Chemicals produced by the butterfly or moth are responsible for the pigments.

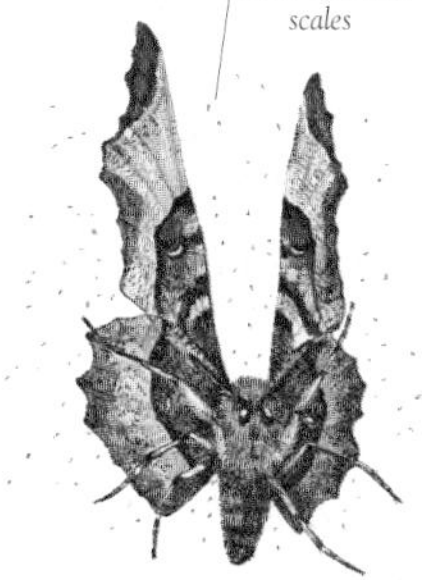

Moth shedding scales

SLIDING SCALES
Each time a butterfly or moth flaps its wings, some of the powderlike scales fall off. Often, the age of a moth or butterfly can be estimated by how many scales have been lost.

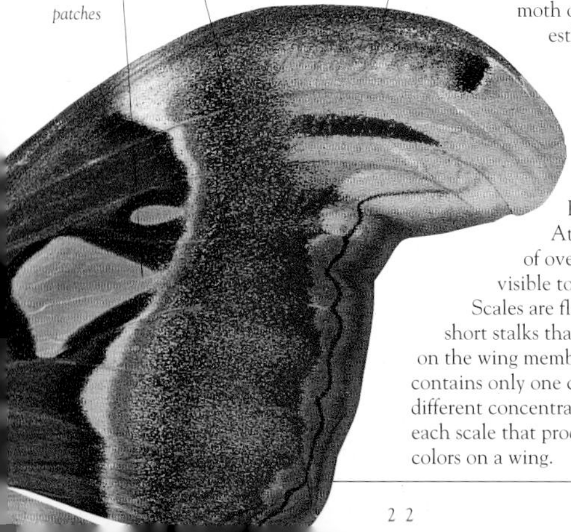

Translucent patches

Powderlike scales

Pigmentary color

ATLAS MOTH

LOOKING CLOSER
At close range, the rows of overlapping scales are visible to the naked eye. Scales are flat, platelike hairs on short stalks that fit into tiny pockets on the wing membrane. Each scale contains only one color. It is the different concentration of pigment in each scale that produces the variety of colors on a wing.

Wings without scales

Some butterflies and moths, such as the Esmeralda Butterfly or the Bumble Bee Sphinx moth, have no scales on large areas of their wings. Bumble Bee Sphinx moths have scales when they hatch from the pupa, but these fall off during the first flight and are known as deciduous scales. Many moths with transparent wings mimic bees.

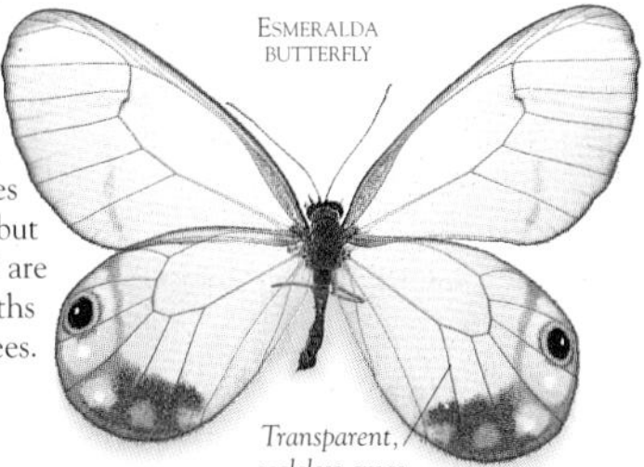

Esmeralda butterfly

Transparent, scaleless areas on wings

Brazilian morpho wing

Metallic blue

Shimmering wings

The iridescent blue colors of this Morpho wing result from the way light is reflected or broken up by specially structured scales on the wing. These scales, which are arranged in layers, catch the light to produce different shades of blue.

Schulze's agrius butterfly

Male disperses scent when courting the female

Androconia on hindwing

Releasing scent

Some scales, called androconia, are modified for dispersing scent. They are usually long and slender with a tuft of fine hairs at the tip. Androconia are connected to scent glands in the wing membrane, and scent is released up through the hollow scales into the air.

SENSES

BUTTERFLIES AND MOTHS rely on their senses for survival. Their bodies are covered with sensory hairs that, according to the position on the body, respond to different sensations – smell, taste, and touch. Butterflies and moths have compound eyes that are linked to nerves inside the body.

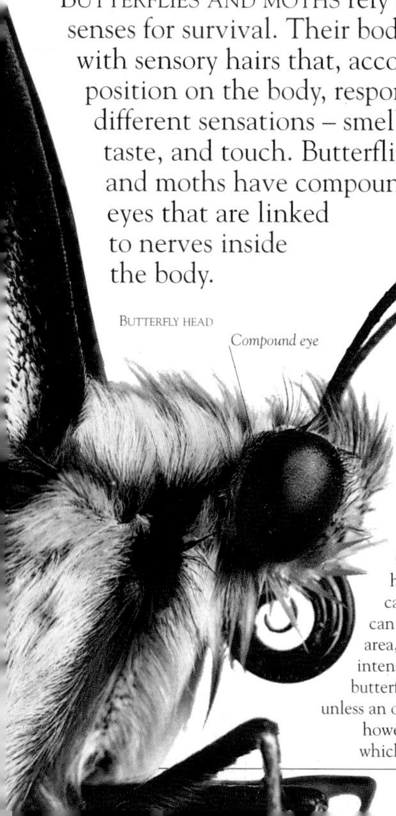
Compound eye
BUTTERFLY HEAD

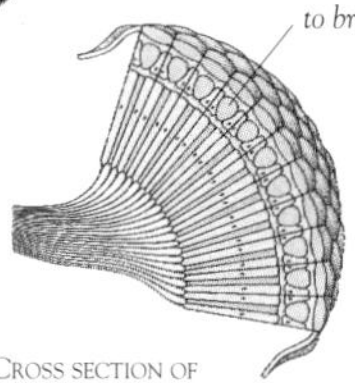
Each ommatidium i
linked to a nerve
that sends messages
to brain
CROSS SECTION OF COMPOUND EYE

SIGHT

Compound eyes consist of hundreds or thousands of lenses called ommatidia. This type of eye can pick up movement over a wide area, and can also detect light intensity and color. Moths and butterflies cannot focus on details unless an object is very close. They can, however, detect ultraviolet light, which humans cannot see.

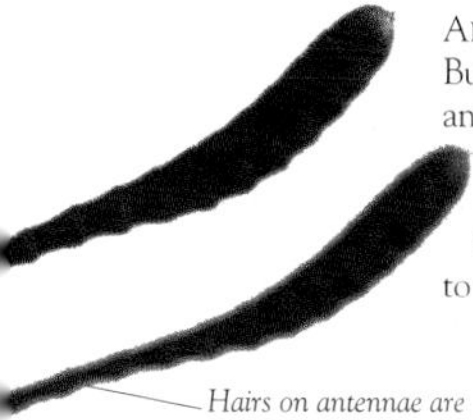

ANTENNAE

Butterflies and moths do not have noses, but their antennae are very sensitive to smells. The antennae of some male moths are feathery, providing a large surface area for picking up the odors given off by females trying to attract a mate. Antennae are sensitive to touch, taste, temperature, and wind movement.

Hairs on antennae are particularly sensitive to scent and touch

Ears alert moth to danger

NOCTUID MOTH

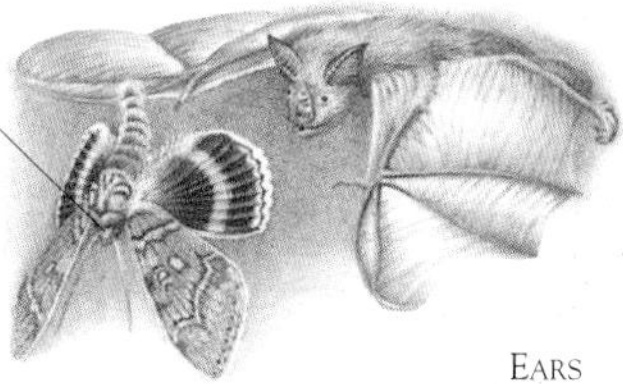

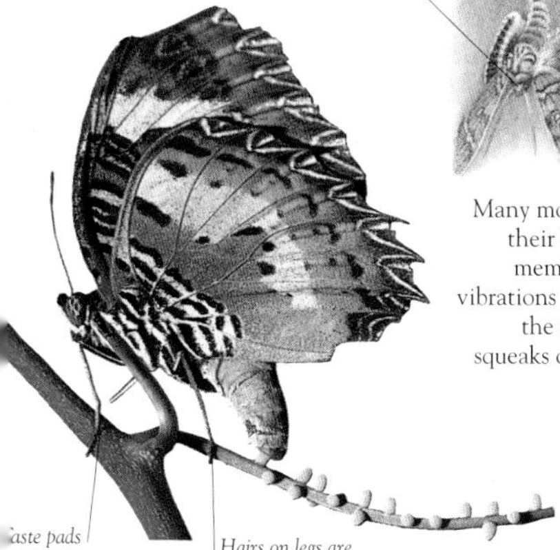

EARS

Many moths have ears on the sides of their bodies. These consist of thin membranes, which pick up sound vibrations from the air. At night, when the moths hear the high-pitched squeaks of bats, they dodge out of the way to avoid being eaten.

aste pads on feet

Hairs on legs are sensitive to touch

MALAY LACEWING LAYING HER EGGS

TASTING WITH FEET

When a female butterfly is ready to lay her eggs, she uses the taste pads on her feet to find plants that the caterpillars can eat. Young caterpillars are too small to crawl far and need to find nourishment quickly or they will die.

SENSES FACTS

- Some moths have additional simple eyes (ocelli).
- A male Emperor moth can smell a female up to 6 miles (10 km) away.
- The antennae of some moths are 5 times the length of their wings.

Feeding and drinking

Most adult butterflies and moths suck up liquid food through their strawlike proboscis. The most common food is sweet flower nectar, but some species feed on tree sap, rotting fruit, animal droppings, flui around the eyes of living animals, and even fresh blood. A few moths hav jaws to chew flow pollen.

PROBOSCIS
The length of the proboscis varies in different species to suit the flowers on which the insect feeds. The proboscis of the Madagascan Morgan's Sphinx moth is far longer than its body. It penetrates deep inside the flower to reach the hidden nectar.

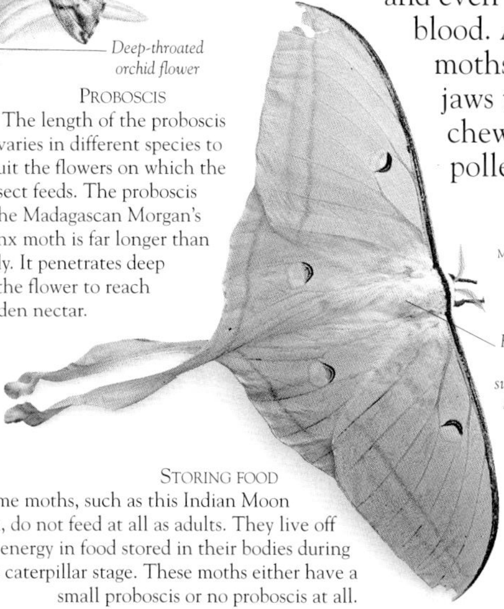

STORING FOOD
Some moths, such as this Indian Moon moth, do not feed at all as adults. They live off the energy in food stored in their bodies during the caterpillar stage. These moths either have a small proboscis or no proboscis at all.

ABSORBING MINERALS

utterflies often gather in large groups : muddy puddles or on damp ground, specially in hot countries where water scarce. As they drink, they absorb aluable mineral salts and other nutrients. he salts are important for male eproductive development.

Group of Sulphurs drink water from damp ground

ONEY DIET

emarkable for the skull-like marking its thorax, the Death's Head awkmoth feeds on honey. Its ort, strong, muscular proboscis ideal for piercing the neycomb in a beehive reach the honey inside.

UIT JUICE

otting fruit is a popular eal for many butterflies d moths, including this wl butterfly. As the fruit s, it breaks down into uids. The butterfly stes the juices with two outhparts, called palps, the base of its proboscis.

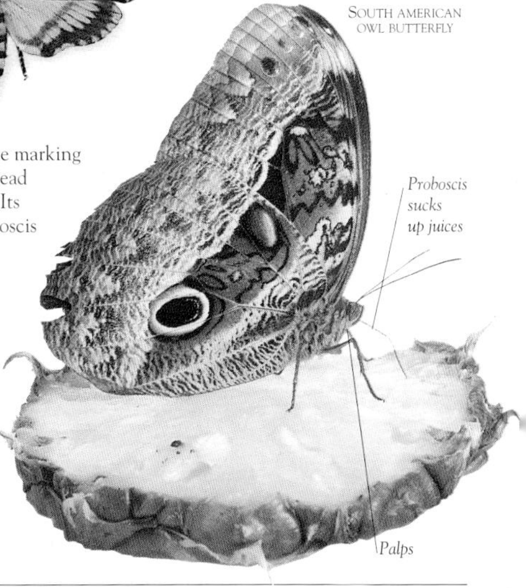

LIFE CYCLE

THERE ARE FOUR distinct stages in the life of a butter or moth – egg, caterpillar, pupa, and adult. The who process of change is called complete metamorphosis. The length of each phase depends on the species anc climate. A life cycle in the tropics might last about three weeks, while in colder climates, it may last several months or longer.

STAGE 1 – EGG
Eggs, the size of pinheads, are usually laid singly or in clusters on or near the plant on which the caterpillar will feed. Each species has a different egg, distinctively shaped and marked. The colors of the egg may darken before hatching.

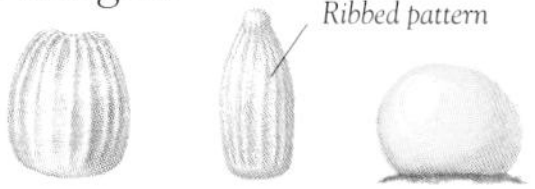

Ribbed pattern

PAINTED LADY EGG

LARGE WHITE BUTTERFLY EGG

SWALLOWTAIL EGG

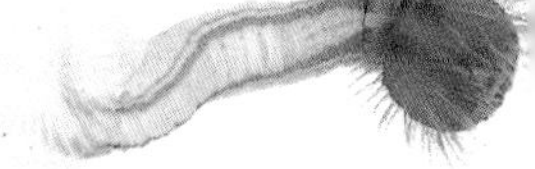

Caterpillar emerging fro transparent

OWL BUTTEF LARVA

STAGE 2 – CATERPILLAR
The caterpillar, or larva, eats voraciously from the moment it bites through its eggshell. During this stage, a caterpillar may grow to many times its original size before it is ready to become a pupa.

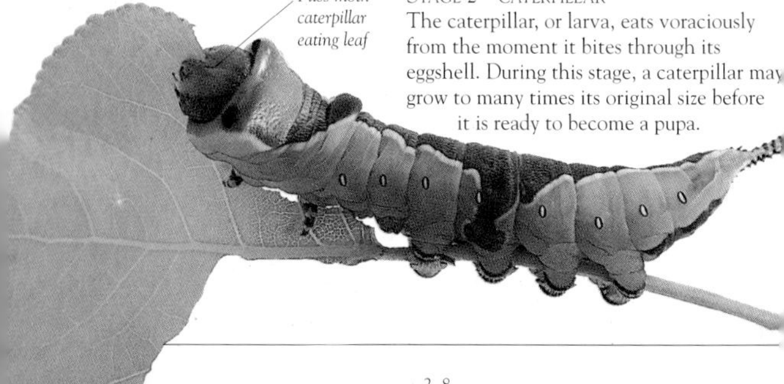

Puss moth caterpillar eating leaf

STAGE 3 – PUPA
Within the hard, protective case of a pupa, the caterpillar is transformed into an adult. The pupa appears almost lifeless – it does not feed and rarely moves – but within the case there is plenty of activity. The body of the larva is liquefied and the cells are reorganized into the features of the adult.

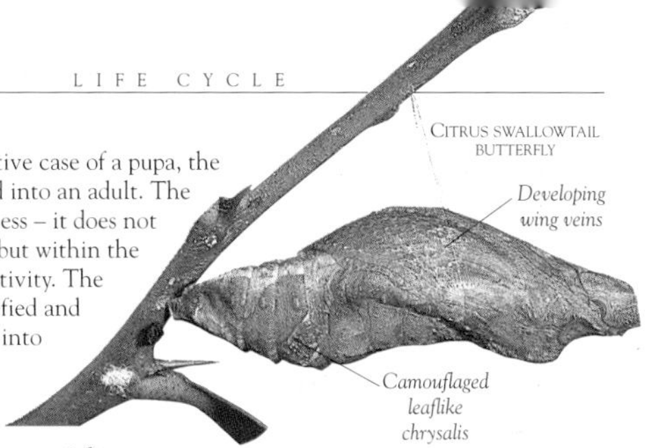

CITRUS SWALLOWTAIL BUTTERFLY

Developing wing veins

Camouflaged leaflike chrysalis

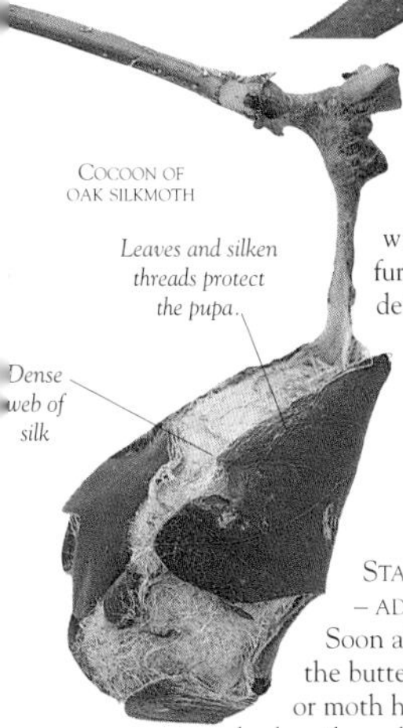

COCOON OF OAK SILKMOTH

Leaves and silken threads protect the pupa.

Dense web of silk

PROTECTING THE PUPA
Since the pupa cannot move, the insect is vulnerable to predators. The color and shape of a butterfly pupa, or chrysalis, are adapted to blend with a pupa's surroundings. Moth pupae are often further protected inside a cocoon of silk or plant debris, such as leaves and twigs.

COURTING PASSION-VINE BUTTERFLIES

STAGE 4 – ADULT
Soon after the butterfly or moth has broken through the pupal case, it flies off in search of a mate. A vital role of the adult is to mate and disperse its eggs to ensure the survival of its species. Adults do not grow, and if they feed, it is only to replace the energy they have used up by flying around.

Courtship and mating

When ready to mate, the adult butterfly or moth has to find a mate of the same species. Butterflies and moths must usually look, feel, and smell right to each other before mating can take place. They are attracted by the particular colors and patterns of their own species, and by scented chemical substances called pheromones. Butterflies and moths release these perfumed signals when they are ready to mate.

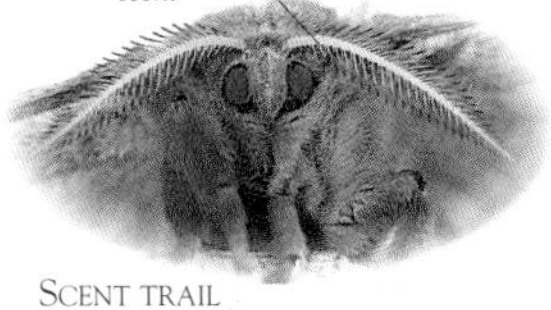

Feathery antenna of moth detects scent

SCENT TRAIL

Night-flying moths cannot use color to attract and recognize a mate. Instead, the male uses his sensitive antennae to pick up the perfumed trail of pheromones left by the female. Each species has a different scent.

Brightly coloured male

Larger wings of female

CRAMER'S BLUE MORPHOS

SEX DIFFERENCES

Male and female butterflies often have different colors, like these Central American butterflies. Males tend to be more colorful, but females are usually larger than males. The wings of the male reflect ultraviolet light, which the females can see but we cannot.

Female
\bdomens join
)gether so male
can fertilize
female's eggs
Male claspers
hold female's body
Male

SWALLOWTAILS

MATING

Both butterflies and moths mate end to end, with the male and female facing in opposite directions. Once they are joined, the pair may fly together, keeping out of sight of predators. Mating can last from 20 minutes to a few hours.

.AYING EGGS

.fter mating, the male flies off) find another female and the :male searches for a plant on hich to lay her eggs. When ıe finds a plant on which the aterpillar will feed, she sticks er eggs firmly to the plant r to a nearby object with secretion from her body. pecies that feed on a wide .nge of plants may scatter ;gs over them in flight.

Cinnabar moth laying eggs

Caterpillar growth

Many caterpillars, or larvae, hatch out of their eggs after about a week, but some remain in their shells for several months over winter. Caterpillars eat voraciously, growing quickly and building up energy supplies for use later in the life cycle. Unlike the adults caterpillars do not have a liquid diet and use biting mouthparts, instead of a proboscis, to feed. Although caterpillars can strip a tree of all its leaves, they are very particular about the plants they will eat. If no suitable plant is available, caterpillars will starve to death rather than eat anything else.

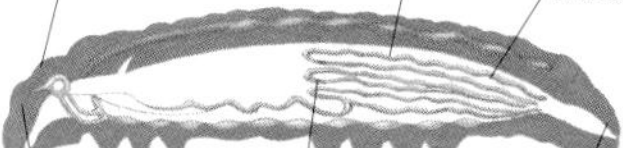

INSIDE A CATERPILLAR
The caterpillar's digestive system consists of a tube that leads from the mouth to the anus at the tip of the abdomen. Waste food is pushed out of the anus as small, hard pellets known as frass.

CROW SWALLOWTA
CATERPILLAR

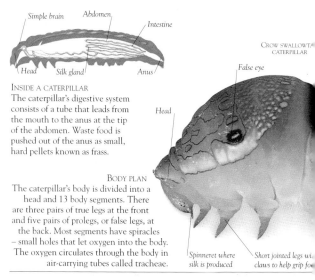

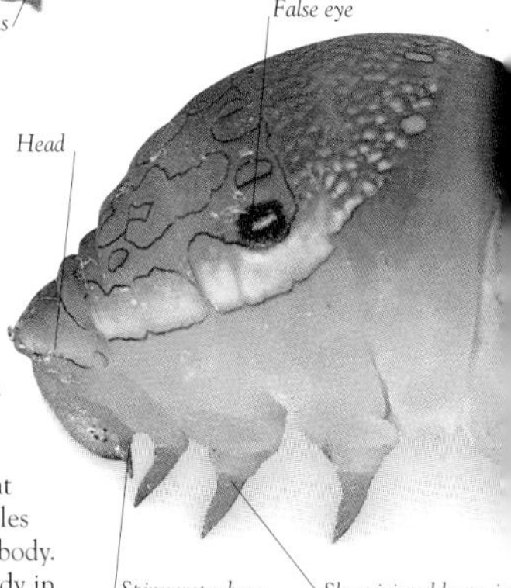

BODY PLAN
The caterpillar's body is divided into a head and 13 body segments. There are three pairs of true legs at the front and five pairs of prolegs, or false legs, at the back. Most segments have spiracles – small holes that let oxygen into the body. The oxygen circulates through the body in air-carrying tubes called tracheae.

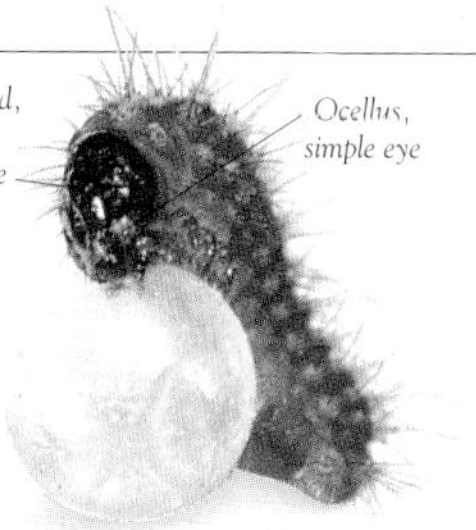

MOTH CATERPILLAR

HATCHING OUT

This moth caterpillar has bitten its way out of the egg. Eating the eggshell gives the growing caterpillar the nutrients it needs.

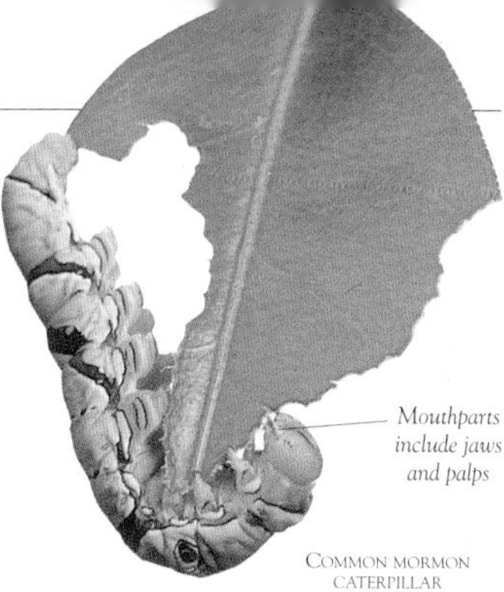

COMMON MORMON CATERPILLAR

FEEDING

Caterpillars bite off pieces of leaf with their powerful mandibles (jaws). Sensory organs, called palps, are used to taste the food to ensure that it is suitable to eat, and the mandibles shred it into pieces.

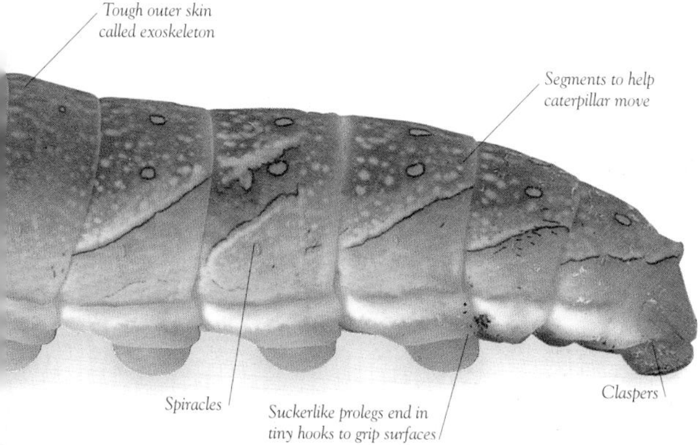

Developing and moving

The tough, flexible covering on the outside of a caterpillar's body allows it to wriggle and crawl, but will not stretch enough for it to grow. Every so often, the caterpillar has to molt, or shed its old skin. This process, called ecdysis, usually happens four or five tim during a caterpillar's life. While molting, larvae often spin silken pads to fix themselves to plants. Unlike the adults, caterpillars can produce silk.

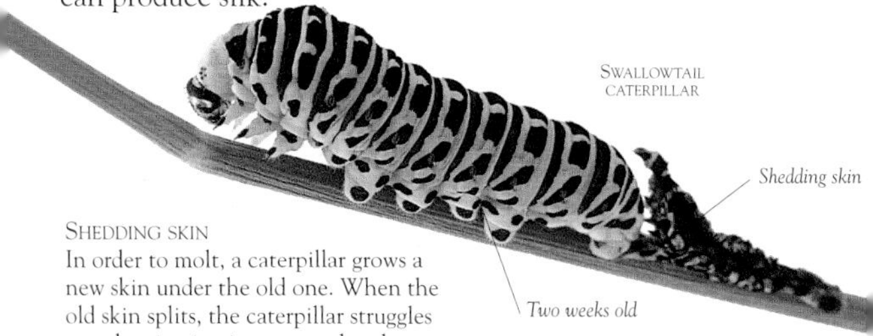

SWALLOWTAIL CATERPILLAR

SHEDDING SKIN

In order to molt, a caterpillar grows a new skin under the old one. When the old skin splits, the caterpillar struggles out, drawing in air to expand and stretch its body. It cannot feed for several hours, until the new skin and mouth harden.

SOUTH AMERICAN OWL BUTTERFLY CATERPILLAR

COLOR CHANGE

The color of a caterpillar's skin may change as it molts. This Owl butterfly caterpillar from South America has a green skin when youn and a brown skin when it is older.

'angling from
trong thread
of silk

OAK LEAF-ROLLER
CATERPILLAR

SILKEN LIFELINE

Many caterpillars, such as this Oak Leaf-roller caterpillar, use a silken line to escape predators. They drop from a branch or a leaf, holding tightly to the end of the silk and may spin around so fast that they become almost invisible. When the danger has passed, the caterpillars climb up the silk and start feeding again.

'lk protects
pupa

OAK SILKMOTH
CATERPILLAR

SPINNING SILK

Moth caterpillars often spin a silken cocoon to protect their pupae. Caterpillars produce silk from a gland in the body, and the silk threads are drawn out by spinnerets under the head. The silk is liquid at first, but soon hardens when it meets the air.

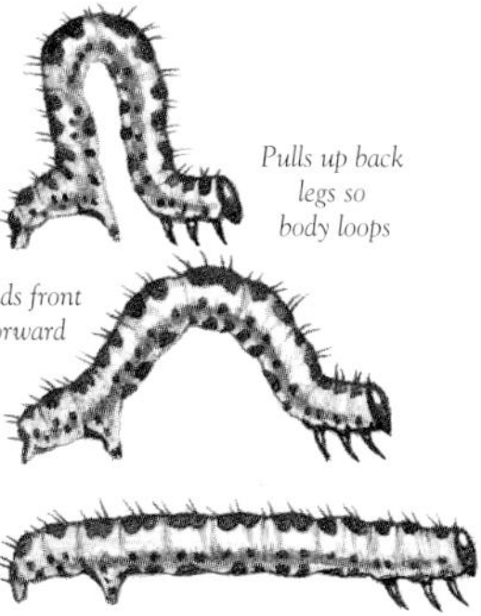

Pulls up back legs so body loops

Extends front legs forward

Stretches body out flat

LOOPER CATERPILLAR

Caterpillars of the moth family Geometridae have fewer prolegs than other caterpillars, and the middle part of :he body has no legs at all. They are often called Looper caterpillars or Inchworms because of the way they move. The ıterpillars appear to advance inch by inch by repeatedly arching their bodies into a loop.

Caterpillar to adult

When a caterpillar is fully grown, it finds a suitable place to change into a pupa (pupate) and then sheds its skin for the last time. Inside the protective case of the pupa, an amazing transformation takes place. All the parts of the caterpillar's body are broken down into their various components, which then develop to mak the body and wings of the adult. Some of the changes can be seen through the pupal skin. The time it takes to change into an adult varies from weeks to months, depending on the climate and species.

CHANGE
The larva of this Swallowtail butterfly is preparing to pupate. It spins a silken loop for support and hangs from a stem. Soon, its skin will split along the back, revealing the green pupa inside.

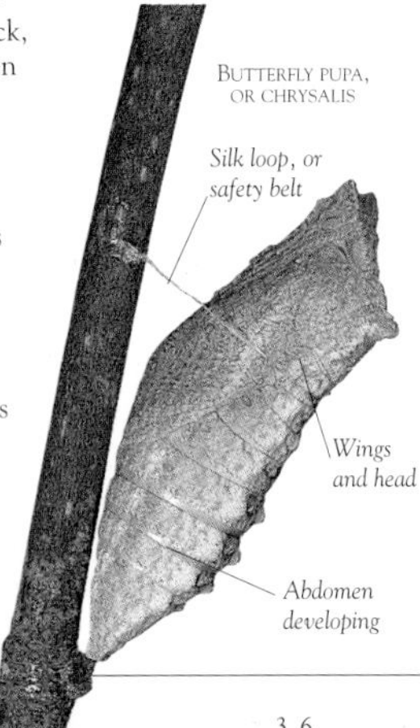

BUTTERFLY PUPA, OR CHRYSALIS

BUILDING BODIES
The pupa darkens and hardens on contact with the air to protect the developing butterfly. All parts of the adult body begin to take shape. The pupa can be either green or brown to match its surroundings.

UNDERGROUND PUPA
Some moths, such as th Sphinx moth, pupate underground, where the are safer from predators. The caterpillar hollows out a chamber and bind the walls with saliva an strands of silk.

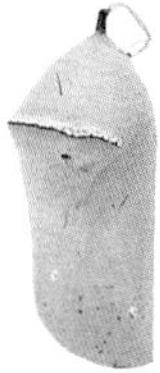

QUEEN BUTTERFLY PUPA

CRUISER BUTTERLY PUPA

FREAK BUTTERFLY PUPA

PUPAE

Many caterpillars pupate above ground; their pupae are often camouflaged for protection. While gold spots distract predators, bright colors warn them that the pupa is poisonous. Since a pupa cannot feed or drink, some pupae have a waxy surface to reduce water loss.

OLD WORLD SWALLOWTAIL

Butterfly pushes its way out of split pupa

THE NEW BUTTERFLY

When the butterfly first emerges from the chrysalis (butterfly pupa), its wings are wrinkled, wet, and only a fraction of their eventual size. It sits still while blood pumps through the wing veins to stiffen and flatten the wings.

Pull of gravity helps stretch wings of upside-down butterfly

NEW WINGS

It may take two hours or more for a large butterfly to fully expand and dry its wings, but for smaller species, the process is much shorter. Once the wings are dry, the butterfly usually flies off to the nearest flower to feed.

SURVIVAL

Common Blue butterfly being eaten by spider

WITHOUT SHARP TEETH, claws, or stings to defend themselves, moths and butterflies rely on more subtle means of protection. These range from camouflage to bright colors that warn predators they are poisonous. Caterpillars may have sharp spines or irritating hairs, or mimic harmful creatures and inedible objects.

PREDATORS
Often attacked by birds and spiders, moths and butterflies are also threatened by small mammals and lizards. Moths that fly at night to avoid birds may be eaten by bats instead.

FALSE EYES
Eyespots on the wings fool predators into thinking that the head is on the wings. A butterfly or moth can still fly with parts of its wings missing, but an injury to the head or body is usually fatal.

Eyespots on edge of wings – far away from body

PAPILIO PALINURUS SWALLOWTAIL

Insect disguise

When the caterpillar of the Lobster Moth is threatened, it lifts up its head and scorpion-like tail to make itself look fierce. Young Lobster Moth caterpillars resemble red ants and often gather together on branches.

Lobster Moth caterpillar

Red underwing moth

Shock tactics

Some moths and butterflies have bright patches of color or false eyes hidden away on their hind wings. If danger threatens, they quickly spread their wings and flash their colors or eyespots to startle an attacker.

Zebra caterpillar

Caterpillar weapons

The Zebra caterpillar becomes poisonous through eating poisonous plants. It also has sharp spines to protect its soft body. Other caterpillars have irritating or poisonous hairs. A few caterpillars look like small snakes – they have large, false eyes and shake their heads vigorously from side to side when threatened.

Camouflage

Many butterflies and moths use camouflage to defend themselves from predators. Some species resemble inanimate objects such as twigs or dead leaves; others may be colored to match their backgrounds, or they may have patterns on their wings that help break up their body shape.

Camouflage is used as a survival technique throughout the life cycle and is most effective when the insect keeps still.

PEPPERED MOTH CATERPILLAR

Scars and bud-like marking

TWIG MIMIC

This caterpillar rests at an angle, projecting itself from the main twig. When resting, the caterpillar is difficult to detect, since it mimics the color, texture, and shape of the twig. But any movement to find food makes it visible.

Larvae of tropical Swallowtail butterflies

Larvae mimicking bird droppings

INEDIBLE

By mimicking bird droppings, these caterpillars trick birds into leaving them alone. Some larvae, such as Japanese Swallowtail caterpillars, start out by looking like bird droppings but, as they grow larger, they adapt their disguise to their increased size. Japanese Swallowtail larvae eventually resemble small snakes.

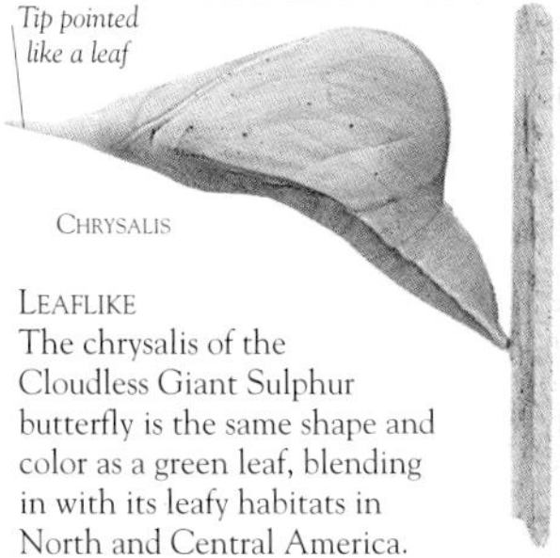

Tip pointed like a leaf

CHRYSALIS

LEAFLIKE

The chrysalis of the Cloudless Giant Sulphur butterfly is the same shape and color as a green leaf, blending in with its leafy habitats in North and Central America. Since pupae are unable to move, camouflage is their best means of defense.

Speckled form

PEPPERED MOTH

Black form is common in polluted areas

ENVIRONMENTAL CHANGE

Night-flying moths that rest by day are often especially well camouflaged. In some industrial areas, speckled Peppered Moths have been replaced by darker-colored Peppered Moths. These blend more effectively with tree trunks darkened by pollution.

.EAF BUTTERFLY

\ number of caterpillars, ›upae, and adults mimic lry, dead, curled-up leaves. \ few butterflies, such as his Indian Leaf Butterfly, .re remarkable for heir similarity to a 'ried leaf. The wings .re shaped like eaves, with ointed tips to esemble stems, nd there are lines n the undersides hat look like the eins of a leaf.

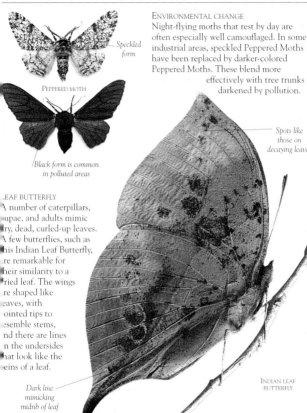

Spots like those on decaying leaves

Dark line mimicking midrib of leaf

INDIAN LEAF BUTTERFLY

Warning colors and mimicry

Some moths and butterflies are brightly colored to warn predators that they are poisonous. Others confuse predators by mimicking harmful creatures. Some harmless butterflies mimic the warning colors of poisonous species; common warning colors are red, orange, yellow, and black. In some species, only the females are mimics, since they need extra protection if they are to survive and lay eggs.

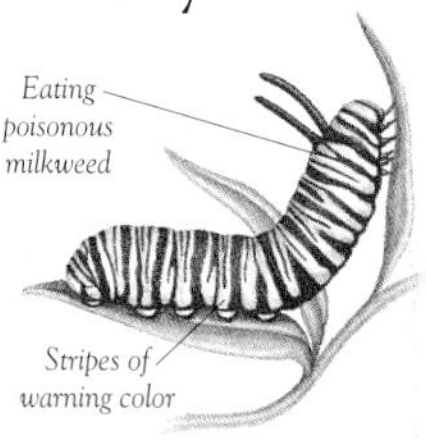

EATING POISONS
Some caterpillars, such as Monarch larvae, become poisonous from eating toxic plants. They store the poisons in their body.

MONARCH BUTTERFLY

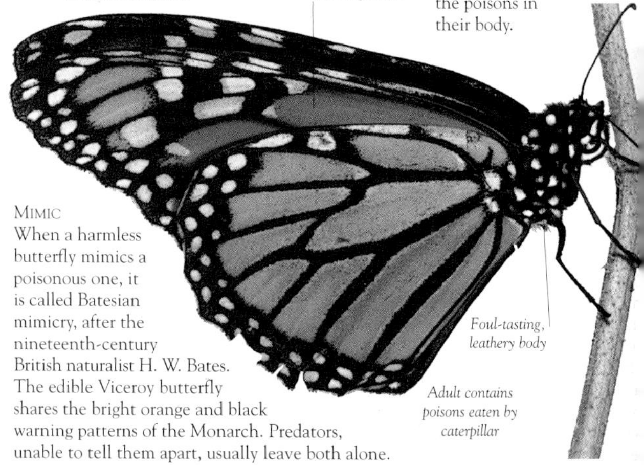

MIMIC
When a harmless butterfly mimics a poisonous one, it is called Batesian mimicry, after the nineteenth-century British naturalist H. W. Bates. The edible Viceroy butterfly shares the bright orange and black warning patterns of the Monarch. Predators, unable to tell them apart, usually leave both alone.

POSTMAN BUTTERFLY

)STMAN BUTTERFLY MIMICS

'hen two poisonous species look nilar, it is called Müllerian mimicry. Fritz üller, a German-born Brazilian biologist, scovered the phenomenon in the neteenth century. These two ecies of Postman butterflies share e same warning colors as well similar habitats in Central and outh America. Predators soon arn to avoid all species with e same "uniform."

SMALL POSTMAN

'ASP OR MOTH?

nis Hornet Moth has transparent ngs and a body ringed in yellow and ack like a hornet (a species of large wasp). ther harmless moths also look like bees or asps and even behave in a similar way. ney fly rapidly in bright sunshine, visit owers, and some even buzz as they fly. edators avoid them for fear of being stung.

HORNET MOTH

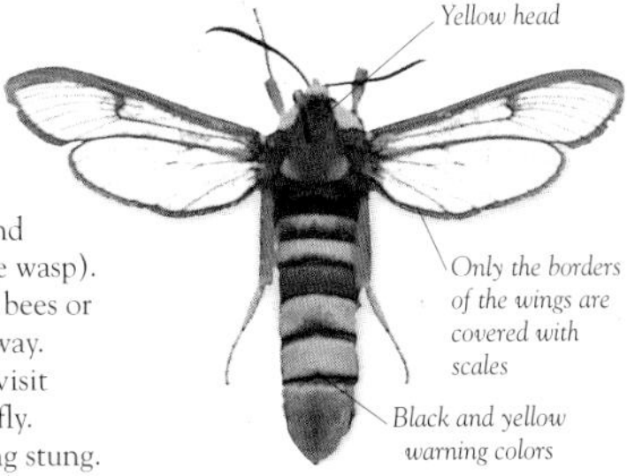

Migration and hibernation

Some butterflies and moths migrate in order to follow food or avoid bad weather or overcrowding. They usually migrate in only one direction from their place of birth to a new area. They may breed en route. Some species survive extreme weather by resting for long periods. This is called hibernation in cold weather and estivation during hot, dry spells.

Monarchs pass winter clinging to pine trees

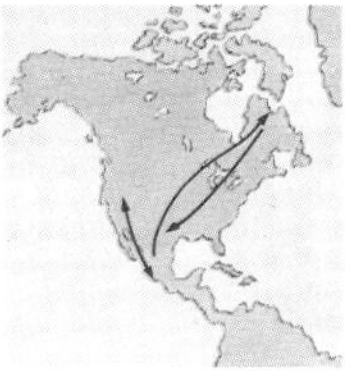

Well-monitored migration routes over America

MONARCH BUTTERFLIES
Every autumn, large groups of Monarchs swarm across North America to hibernate in the mountain forests of southern California or Mexico. In spring, they (or their offspring) return northward alone or in small groups.

PAINTED LADIES
To avoid overcrowding, each spring millions of Painted Ladies follow a variety of migration routes throughout the world. They travel widely but in only one direction, crossing high mountain barriers and breeding en route.

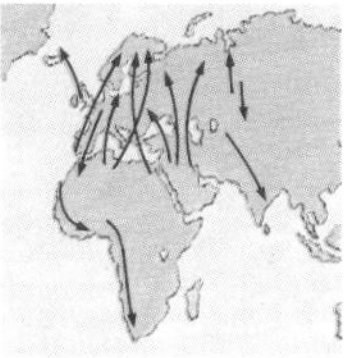

When Painted Ladies travel north from the deserts of Africa, they cross the Alps

PAINTED L
BUTTERFL

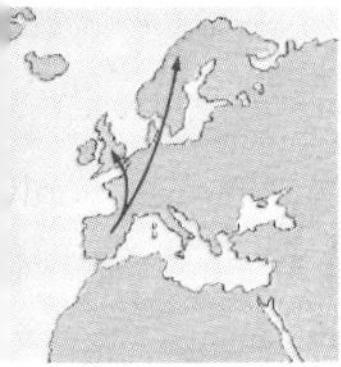

In summer, these Hawkmoths flock through the Pyrenean passes

HUMMINGBIRD HAWKMOTH

MIGRATION FACTS

- Some Painted Ladies can migrate up to 620 miles (1,000 km).
- Swarms of migrating Bogong moths can clog up factory machinery.
- Most migrating butterflies fly at about 20 ft (6 m) above ground; Monarchs fly up to 400 ft (122 m) above ground.

HUMMINGBIRD HAWKMOTHS

These moths are strong fliers, regularly traveling long distances. In spring, they begin their flight from southern Europe to northern Europe, moving northward as the weather becomes warmer.

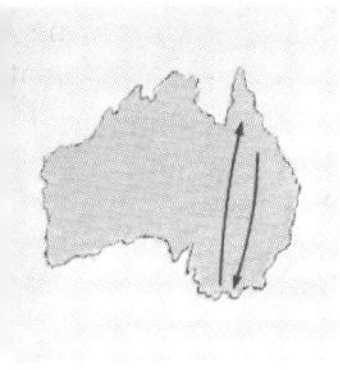

Bogong moths fly north when the weather is cooler

BOGONG MOTH

ESTIVATION

During hot, dry weather, Bogong moths estivate in rock crevices and caves in the Australian Alps. When it gets cooler, they emerge from their dormant state. They fly, in large numbers, northward to low, cultivated land.

HIBERNATION

In temperate regions, butterflies and moths hibernate during the winter when it is too cold for them to move and there are few plants on which to feed. While some species hibernate as adults, others hibernate as eggs, caterpillars, or pupae. At rest, their life processes slow down to conserve energy. They reemerge when the weather is warmer.

Peacock butterflies hanging

FRIENDS AND FOES

ALTHOUGH SOME BUTTERFLIES and moths are serious pests, the vast majority are harmless insects that benefit the environment by pollinating flowers. Some species of caterpillars feed on weeds, and others have been cultivated for centuries for their fine silk, which is sold commercially.

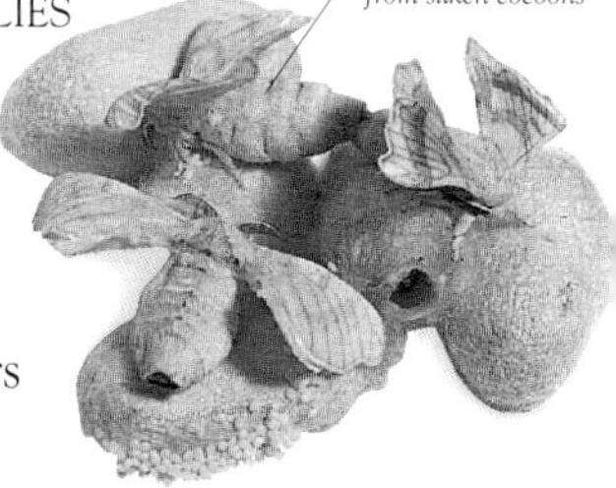

Silkmoths emerging from silken cocoons

SILK PRODUCERS
Silkworms (Silkmoth larvae) spin fine silken threads for their cocoons. They are bred on special farms, where they are fed mulberry leaves. The thread of one caterpillar can be as long as 2,625 ft (800 m).

Proboscis covered with pollen

Butterfly carries pollen from flower to flower

POLLINATION
Flowers have nectar and scent to encourage visits from butterflies and moths. As they drink nectar, dustlike grains of pollen may stick to their bodies. If they feed on another flower of the same kind, the male sex cells in the pollen they carry may fertilize the female sex cells. The plant can then make seeds and reproduce.

Common Clothes moth eating felt

CLOTHES MOTHS

The small, white caterpillars of the Common Clothes moth feed on natural materials, such as wool and fur. The False Clothes moth, or House moth, attacks natural fibres and may even destroy synthetic fibers like nylon and polystyrene.

Destructive Pine Emperor moth

PINE EMPEROR MOTH CATERPILLAR

FOREST PESTS

This caterpillar of the Pine Emperor moth of South Africa can strip pine trees of their leaves, destroying large areas of conifer plantation. In Europe, conifer pests include the larvae of the Pine Processionary moth and the Pine Beauty moth.

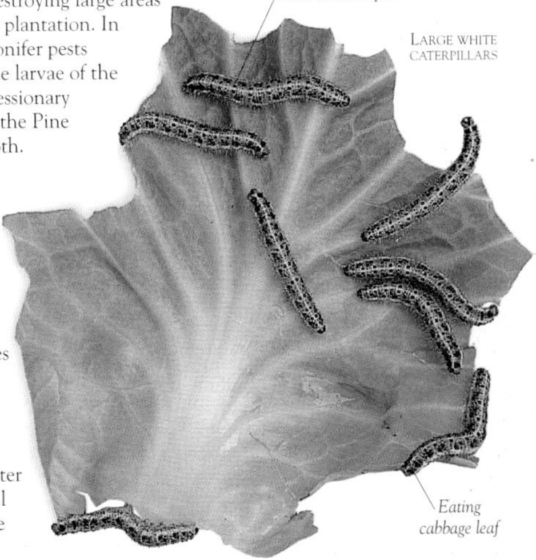

Distinctive stripes

LARGE WHITE CATERPILLARS

Eating cabbage leaf

CABBAGE WHITES

The caterpillars of the Large and the Small White butterflies devour cabbage leaves, rapidly reducing them to skeletons. The Large Whites feed on the outer leaves, while the Small Whites eat away at the heart of the cabbage.

ENVIRONMENTAL CHANGE

BUTTERFLIES AND MOTHS are particularly sensitive to environmental change. If nature's balance is altered, a species can become rare or extinct. The variety of species is threatened by habitat change, by the spread of farmland and urban areas, by pest control programs, and by pollution.

HABITAT DESTRUCTION
This rare species is threatened by the destruction of its rain forest home in Pap New Guinea. Rain forests throughout th world are being destroyed at an alarmin rate since they are a source of timber, farmland, and underground minerals.

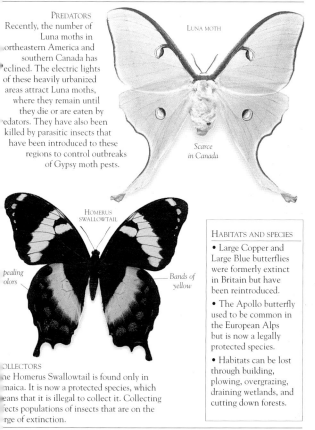

PREDATORS
Recently, the number of Luna moths in ...ortheastern America and southern Canada has ...eclined. The electric lights of these heavily urbanized areas attract Luna moths, where they remain until they die or are eaten by ...edators. They have also been killed by parasitic insects that have been introduced to these regions to control outbreaks of Gypsy moth pests.

...OLLECTORS
...e Homerus Swallowtail is found only in ...maica. It is now a protected species, which ...eans that it is illegal to collect it. Collecting ...ects populations of insects that are on the ...rge of extinction.

HABITATS AND SPECIES

- Large Copper and Large Blue butterflies were formerly extinct in Britain but have been reintroduced.
- The Apollo butterfly used to be common in the European Alps but is now a legally protected species.
- Habitats can be lost through building, plowing, overgrazing, draining wetlands, and cutting down forests.

HABITATS

THE GREATEST VARIETY of butterflies and moths is found in the shelter of tropical rain forests. The warm, humid climate provides a range of food sources. However, butterflies and moths survive in nearly all habitats from hot, dry deserts to frozen Arctic tundra. Many species live in more than one habitat.

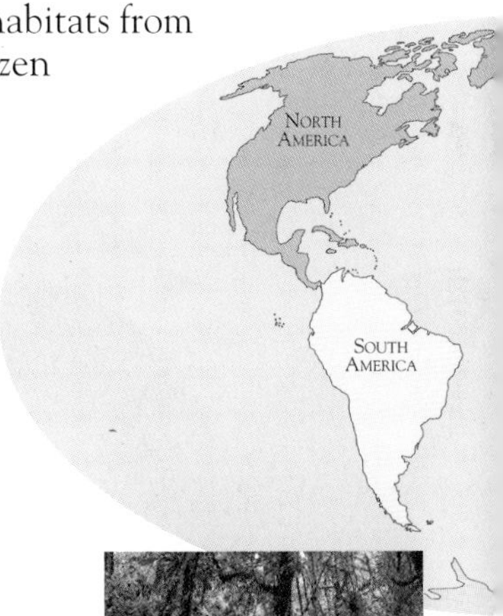

TEMPERATE WOODLANDS
Butterflies and moths prefer sunny clearings in broad-leaved or coniferous woodlands, where there are plenty of flowers on which they can feed. They survive the cold winter season by hibernating.

RAIN FORESTS
The rich plant growth in these hot, wet habitats encourages a remarkable diversity of exotic butterflies and moths.

ARCTIC AND MOUNTAINS
Only the hardiest of species can live at high altitudes or survive the extreme cold and winds of the Arctic tundra. However, mountain meadows and forests provide shelter and food plants.

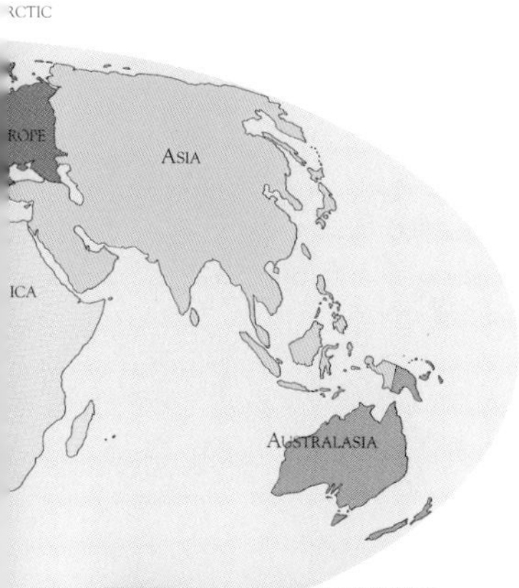

DRY REGIONS AND CAVES
Few moths and butterflies are attracted to the inhospitable habitats created by low rainfall. Caves can provide a refuge during very hot or cold weather.

WETLANDS
The waterlogged soils near seas, rivers, and lakes provide a range of food plants suitable for some moths and butterflies.

GRASSLANDS AND BARRENS
From coastal lowlands to tropical savanna, these habitats provide a variety of grasses and wildflowers to attract moths and butterflies. However, there is little shelter from winds and bad weather.

TEMPERATE WOODLANDS

ABOUT THE HABITAT

TEMPERATE WOODLANDS have plenty of food plants and egg-laying sites for butterflies and moths. Some species are restricted to one type of woodland and many caterpillars can eat only certain woodland plants. Butterflies and moths favor sunny forest lanes and clearings rich in wild flowers.

WOODLAND LAYERS
Most butterflies and moths fly back and forth between the various layers of woodland to feed, seek a mate, or escape a predator.

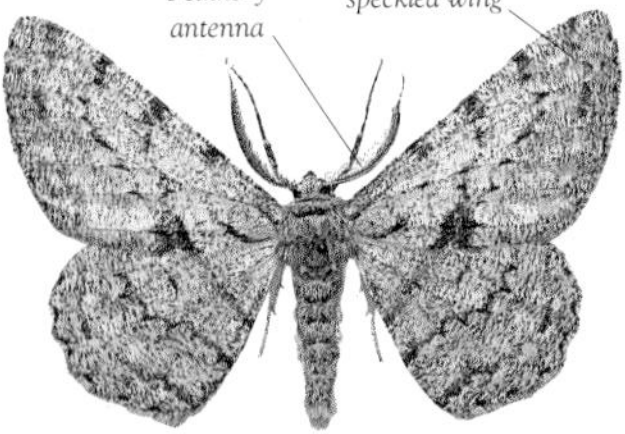

GREAT OAK BEAUTY MOTH

SPECKLED WOOD BUTTERFLY

CAMOUFLAGE
Many woodland butterflies and moths are camouflaged to look like bark or leaves. The colors of the Great Oak Beauty moth blend with the different tree trunks on which it rests. The caterpillars mimic twigs.

TERRITORIAL PATCH
Two male Speckled Wood butterflies may be seen spiraling upward in a sunny clearing. The male who first claimed the clearing as his territory usually manages to chase away the intruder.

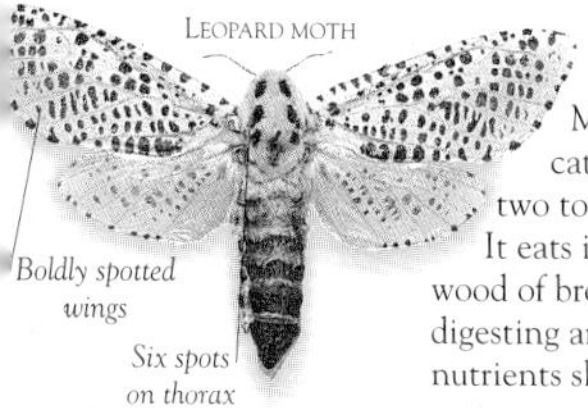

SLOW START

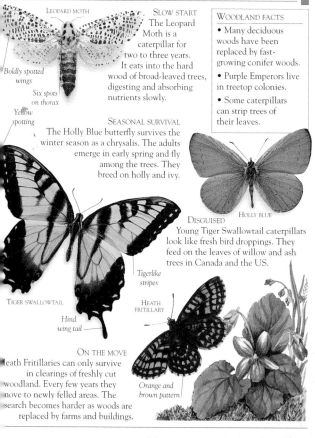

The Leopard Moth is a caterpillar for two to three years. It eats into the hard wood of broad-leaved trees, digesting and absorbing nutrients slowly.

> ### WOODLAND FACTS
>
> - Many deciduous woods have been replaced by fast-growing conifer woods.
> - Purple Emperors live in treetop colonies.
> - Some caterpillars can strip trees of their leaves.

SEASONAL SURVIVAL

The Holly Blue butterfly survives the winter season as a chrysalis. The adults emerge in early spring and fly among the trees. They breed on holly and ivy.

DISGUISED

Young Tiger Swallowtail caterpillars look like fresh bird droppings. They feed on the leaves of willow and ash trees in Canada and the US.

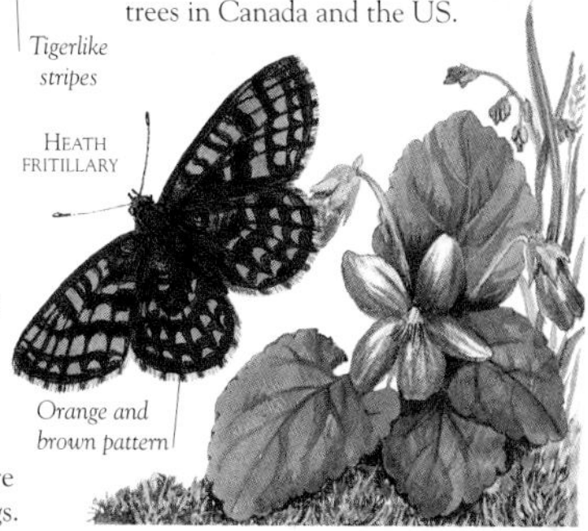

ON THE MOVE

Heath Fritillaries can only survive in clearings of freshly cut woodland. Every few years they move to newly felled areas. The search becomes harder as woods are replaced by farms and buildings.

CONIFER FORESTS

ONLY HARDY SPECIES OF butterflies and moths can survive the cold climate of conifer forests, which grow primarily in northern temperate regions. Many of the trees, such as fir, spruce, and pine, are evergreen and have needle-like leaves that are able to withstand the long, cold winters.

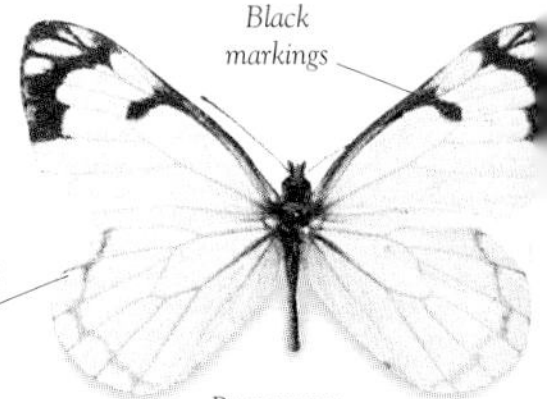

PINE WHITE

PINE PEST
High among fir and pine trees, adult Pine White butterflies flutter weakly. They may descend to the forest floor to feed in the early morning or late afternoon. Their striped caterpillars look like pine needles and can be very destructive to pine woods.

FOLLOWING A THREAD
During the day, Pine Processionary moth larvae rest together in silken webs. At night, they set off in a lon line to look for food. The hea caterpillar spins a silken thread for the others to follow. Each caterpillar branches off to eat but return to the nest guided by a thread of silk.

BLACK
ARCHES MOTH

DISPERSAL

Young caterpillars of the Black Arches moth parachute from the tops of trees, using silken threads. Carried by gusts of wind, they are dispersed throughout the forest.

GYPSY MOTH

IMPORTED

Gypsy moths, originally from Europe and Asia, escaped from a laboratory in America in the 19th century. They have become serious pests in North American forests.

PINE EMPEROR MOTH

Despite its robust appearance, the adult Pine Emperor moth only lives a few days. The adult does not feed and lives off the food that it stored as a caterpillar. When it is ready to pupate, the large, well-fed caterpillar burrows underground.

PINE
EMPEROR
MOTH

BLACK
SPRUCE

PINE-TREE
LAPPET MOTH

IBERNATION

he Pine-tree Lappet moth caterpillar feeds n pine, spruce, fir, and other conifers. It ibernates on the ground and, in spring, ompletes its development in the treetops.

EUCALYPTUS WOODLANDS

IN SOUTHEASTERN and southwestern Australia, butterflies and moths thrive among eucalyptus trees and flowering shrubs. Many of the species are unique to Australia.

ANT FOOD

The caterpillars of the beautiful Common Imperial Blue live in groups and feed on species of wattle. Black ants feed on the sugary substances that the caterpillars secrete.

GIANT ANTHELID

BAT MOTH

Female Giant Anthelids are the size of small bats, with a wingspan of up to 6 ¼ in (16 cm). The large, bristly caterpillars eat eucalyptus leaves and store up fat in their bodies for use later in the life cycle.

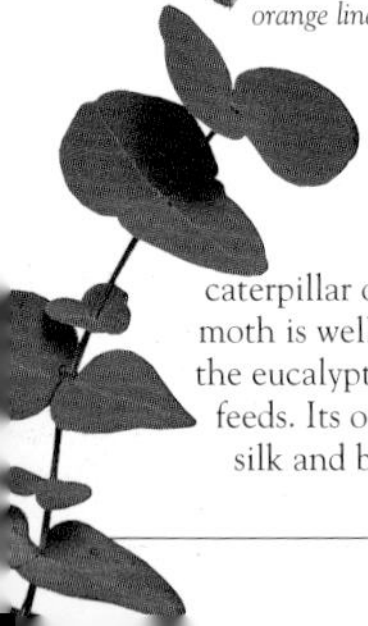

THE GUM EMPEROR MOTH

CAMOUFLAGE

The bluish green caterpillar of the Gum Emperor moth is well camouflaged among the eucalyptus leaves on which it feeds. Its oval cocoon, spun from silk and bark, hangs disguised on eucalyptus trunks.

AUSTRALIAN SKIPPER

The Eastern Flat Skipper is widely distributed in Australia. It flies early in the morning or at dusk, unless disturbed. During the day, it settles on the underside of leaves. The caterpillars live inside tents made from leaves.

EASTERN FLAT SKIPPER

COMMON BROWN

DIFFERENCES

Found in southwest and southeast Australia, the wet season generation of Common Browns may be a different color from the dry season brood. The female butterflies are larger, and the sexes have different markings on their wings.

YELLOW-SPOT BLUE

WATTLE

ELLOW SPOT

'amed after the yellow ›ots on the forewings, .e Yellow-spot Blue ves only in wooded ›untry in Australia. The 'een caterpillar hides by ıy under leaves on the 'ound and is attended / small, black ants. It nerges at night to feed ı *Pimelea* leaves.

NORTHERN BROADLEAF

BUTTERFLIES AND moths fly in the treetops and the understorys of these damp woods found in Asia, Europe, and North America. Broad-leaved trees, such as oak and birch, shed their leaves in autumn.

CALIFORNIA DOG-FACE
As it flits through the open woodlands, the Califor Dog-face butterfly is sometimes known as the "Flying Pansy." It is the state butterfly fc California.

HORNED DEVILS
This beautiful North American moth pupates underground. Its horned caterpillars are called "Hickory Horned Devils" and feed on various trees including hickory and walnut.

MOURNING CLOAK
This butterfly is called the Mourning Cloak because of its somber colors. The adult hibernates but may sometimes fly on warm, winter days. It emits an audible "click" if a predator comes near.

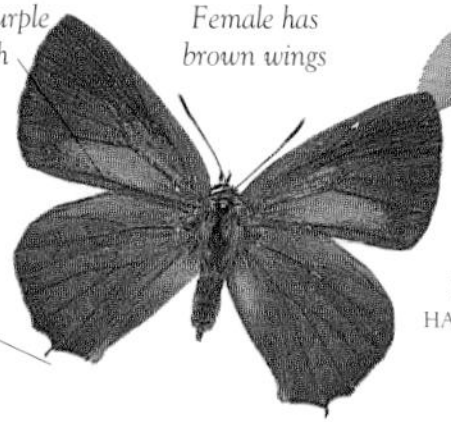

HIGH FLIERS

Purple Hairstreaks keep mainly to the canopy and rarely descend to the ground. The adults feed on the sweet honeydew that aphids secrete on the tree tops. The caterpillars feed on the flower buds and leaves of oak trees.

DISAPPEARING WINGS

When resting on tree trunks, the Woodland Grayling butterfly usually closes its wings. It reveals the barklike pattern on the undersides of its hind wings. The caterpillars hibernate in chambers created out of fallen leaves.

DEAD-LEAF MOTH

At rest, the Poplar Hawkmoth resembles a bunch of dead leaves. If it is disturbed, it flashes the red patches on its wings to startle birds. Caterpillars feed on poplar, willow, alder, and birch trees. They pupate in the soil around the roots of trees.

WOODLAND CLEARINGS

THE GREATEST VARIETY of woodland butterflies and moths is found in grassy open areas such as woodland paths and clearings. While butterflies often bask in the sun, moths usually hide in the undergrowth.

GRASS EATERS

Ringlets flutter amongst the tall, lush grasses of damp, sunny clearings. They are among the few butterflies that can fly in light rain. The larvae can eat only certain grasses.

ON PATROL

The delicate Wood White lives in colonies. Males slowly patrol paths and clearings in search of a mate. Although females fly less, they flit from flower to flower drinking nectar.

WHITE ADMIRALS

These butterflies prefer the shade, gliding swiftly through woodland openings. The females retreat into the forest to lay their glassy, green eggs on the leaves of honeysuckle, the caterpillar's food plant.

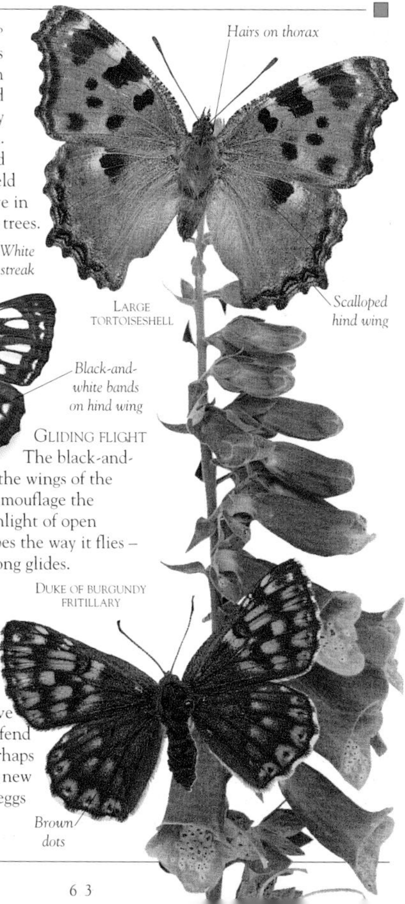

WINTER SLEEP
Adult Large Tortoiseshells overwinter (hibernate) in hollow trees or other sheltered locations. Their long, hairy scales help to keep them warm. In spring, they emerge and sunbathe with their wings held wide open. The caterpillars live in large silken webs on trees.

GLIDING FLIGHT
The black-and-white bands on the wings of the Common Glider help to camouflage the butterfly in the dappled sunlight of open woodland. Its name describes the way it flies – little flits are followed by long glides.

N GUARD
uke of Burgundy Fritillaries live
n small colonies. The males defend
neir territory against rivals, perhaps
erched on a blade of grass in a new
earing. The females lay their eggs
n the undersides of marsh
narigold and primrose leaves.

FRITILLARIES AND CHECKERSPOTS

SPECKLED BUTTERFLIES often fly along forest margins, camouflaged by the dappled sunlight. They may roost in the treetops at night, descending to the woodland floor during the day to feed on bramble or thistle flowers. They appear to have only four legs, since the hairy front legs are too short to be used for walking.

CARDINAL

SUN TRAP
The Cardinal often basks in sunny clearings in southern Europe, North Africa, Iran, and Pakistan, holding its wings at a 45° angle. The beautiful rosy red patch on the underside of its forewings distinguishes it from many other Fritillaries.

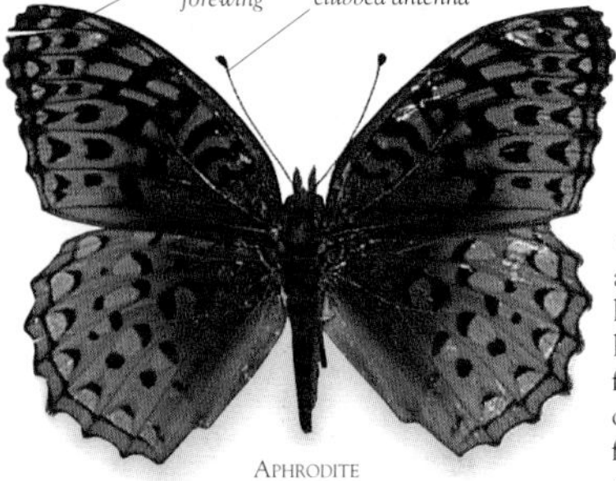

APHRODITE

VIOLET DIET
Female North American Aphrodite butterflies usually lay their eggs directly onto violet leaves in broadleaf and conifer woods. After hatching, the caterpillars hibernate and emerge the following spring. Like many other Fritillary larvae, they feed at night on the leaves of woodland violets.

DOTTED CHECKERSPOT FEMALE

DOTTED CHECKERSPOT MALE

WING PATTERNS
The Dotted Checkerspot from North America has black, orange, and yellow markings. These speckles help to conceal the butterflies in dappled sunlit woods. The undersides of the wings are much paler than the uppersides. The orange caterpillars are protected by orange and black spines.

WASH OF SILVER
Male Silver-washed Fritillaries have black bars on the veins of the forewings, which carry scent scales. The name of this butterfly comes from the wash of silver on the undersides of the hindwings. Silver-washed Fritillaries are unusual in laying their eggs on the bark of trees, such as oaks, near patches of violets.

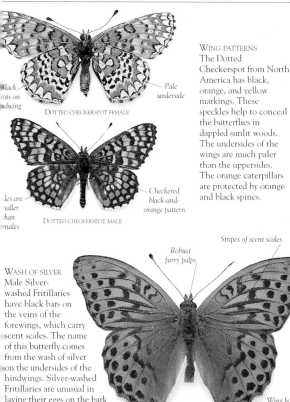

SILVER-WASHED FRITILLARY

TROPICAL RAIN FORESTS

About the Habitat

THE WORLD'S BRIGHTEST and biggest butterflies and moth thrive in the warmth and moisture of the tropical rain forests. Although there is a great diversity of tropical species, their life cycles tend to be short. They are usually active all year round, remaining alert to the many predators that share their rich environment.

RAIN FOREST HABITAT
Tall trees with straight trunks form a leafy canopy. Beneath is an understory of smaller trees, shrubs, and climbing plants. The floor is covered with low-growing plants, fungi, and dead leaves.

BRIGHT COLORS
The bright colors of many rain forest butterflies are surprisingly hard to see in the sun-dappled shadows of the forest. Iridescent colors change in the sunlight, breaking up the shape of the butterfly.

HEWITSON'S BLUE HAIRSTREAK

TAWNY RAJAH

CANOPY

High up in the canopy, butterflies such as Swallowtails, Birdwings, and Morphos abound. The Tawny Rajah flies rapidly in the tree tops to escape bird predators.

RAIN FOREST FACTS

- An area of rain forest the size of a football field is cut down every second.
- Rain forests cover 5% of the Earth's surface.
- Over 50% of all living species live in the tropical rain forests.

CAMOUFLAGE PATTERNS

To make their leaflike camouflage more realistic, no two African Leaf Butterflies are identical. In the wet season when there are fewer dead leaves around, the Leaf Butterflies rely more on eyespots than camouflage to deter predators.

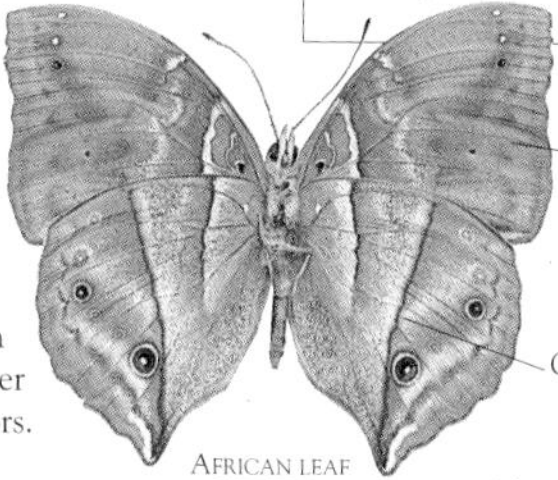

AFRICAN LEAF BUTTERFLY

GLASSWING BUTTERFLY

Glasswing larvae eat passionflower leaves

ORESTFLOOR

Many butterflies and moths shun sunlight, hiding in the darkness of the forest floor. Glasswing butterflies, with their transparent forewings, are almost invisible in the shade. They eat rotting fruit and absorb nutrients from manure or damp ground.

AFRICA

THE SECOND LARGEST AREA of rain forest in the world forms a broad belt across the middle of Africa. The largest butterfly in Africa, *Papilio antimachus*, lives in the tropical rain forests of West Africa; it has a wingspan of up to 10 in (25 cm).

WING MARKINGS
The Common Emperor moth belongs to a small group of orange, brown, and yellow moths that have a translucent patch on each forewing and prominent eyespots on the hindwings.

GREEN MOTH
This striking Sphinx moth is widespread in African rain forests. The caterpillar, which feeds on the leaves of grapevines and Virginia creepers, has eyespots behind its head to deter predators.

POWERFUL FLIERS
Speedy Palla Butterflies are on the wing all year round in the tropical forests of western, eastern, and central Africa. They have short tails on their hind wings.

ɪIANT AFRICAN SKIPPER
'his is probably the largest Skipper
n the world and has a wingspan
f up to 3 ¼ in (8 cm). The
:riking black and white
aterpillar feeds on the
eaves of palm trees.

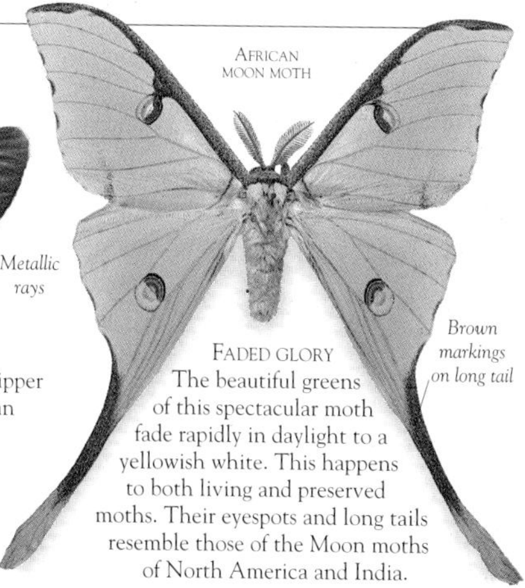

FADED GLORY
The beautiful greens
of this spectacular moth
fade rapidly in daylight to a
yellowish white. This happens
to both living and preserved
moths. Their eyespots and long tails
resemble those of the Moon moths
of North America and India.

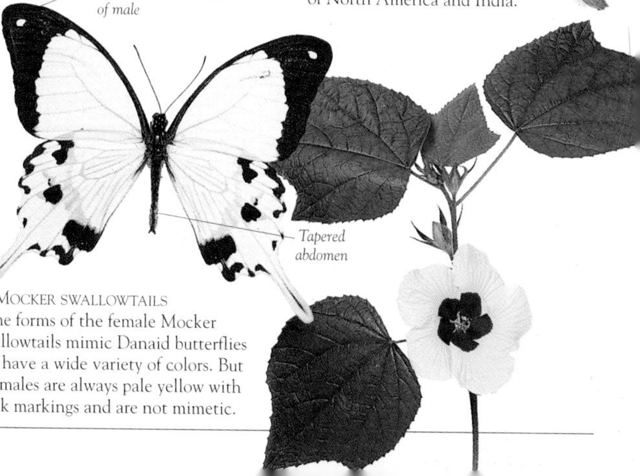

MOCKER SWALLOWTAILS
ɔme forms of the female Mocker
wallowtails mimic Danaid butterflies
ıd have a wide variety of colors. But
ıe males are always pale yellow with
'ack markings and are not mimetic.

ASIA AND AUSTRALASIA

THE HOT, HUMID CLIMATE of southeast Asia, northeast Australia, and Papua New Guinea has encouraged the growth of lush rain forests, where many spectacular butterflies and moths live. Australia and many Asian islands have their own distinct species.

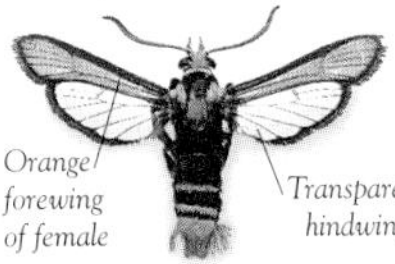

GOLDEN CLEARWING
This wasplike moth from the Northern Territory, Australia, flies quickly in bright sunlight. Males have four transparent wings.

TROPICAL SKIPPER BUTTERFLY
Regent Skippers are unusual both for their bright colors and for the way the males' wings are hooked together like the wings of many moths. They have a swift, jerky flight.

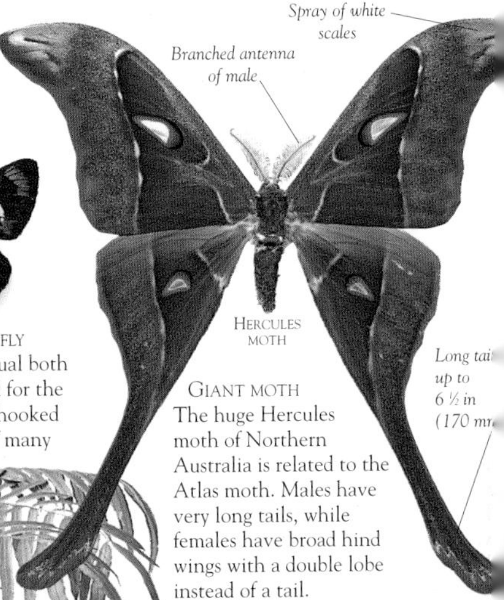

GIANT MOTH
The huge Hercules moth of Northern Australia is related to the Atlas moth. Males have very long tails, while females have broad hind wings with a double lobe instead of a tail.

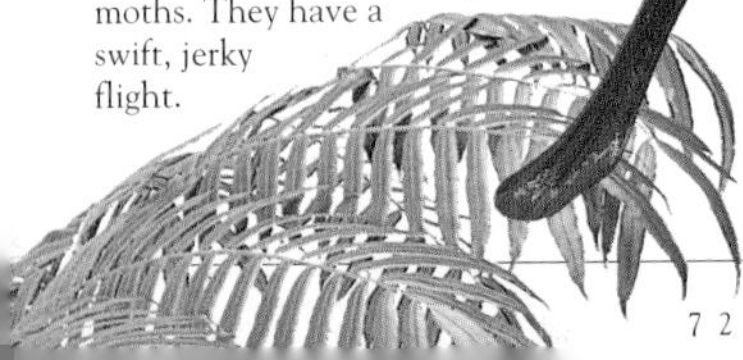

SOARING BIRDWING
Rajah Brooke's Birdwing butterflies have a powerful, soaring flight as they speed through the rain forests of Borneo and Malaysia. The boldly colored males often flock to drink from muddy river banks.

ORANGE SCALES
Waste products react chemically to produce the colors of the Orange Albatross. Males are common on river banks and in forest clearings, but females tend to fly high up in the canopy.

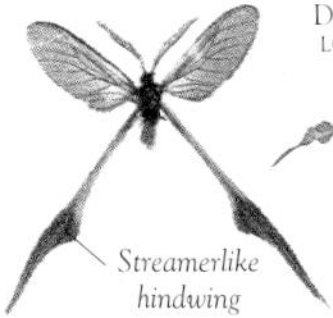

EAD OR ALIVE?
f this strange little moth is listurbed, it drops to the ground and pretends to be lead. Doherty's Longtail is a veak flier, active during the lay in the rain forests of India and Malaysia.

CENTRAL AND SOUTH AMERICA

THE RAIN FORESTS of Central and South America contain the greatest variety of butterfly and moth species in the world, including the stunning Morphos and Owl butterflies. Many of the butterflies and some of the moths have brilliant iridescent colors.

ZEBRA STRIPES
This Zebra butterfly has warning patterns on its long, narrow fore- and hindwings. This species flies slowly in or near dense forests.

DIVA MOTH

Iridescent colors

BLUE THAROPS

DEFENSE TACTICS
The forewings of the larg day-flying Diva Moth are camouflaged like a dead leaf. However, the brightly colored hindwing may flash suddenly to startle a predator.

SHINING WINGS
The fast-flying Blue Tharops butterfly belongs to a group of butterflies called Metalmarks named after the areas of metallic color on their wings.

COLOR MIMIC

Tiger Pierids mimic the bright warning colors of the unpleasant-tasting Danaine butterflies. Their coloring and behavior vary to match the different Danaines they imitate.

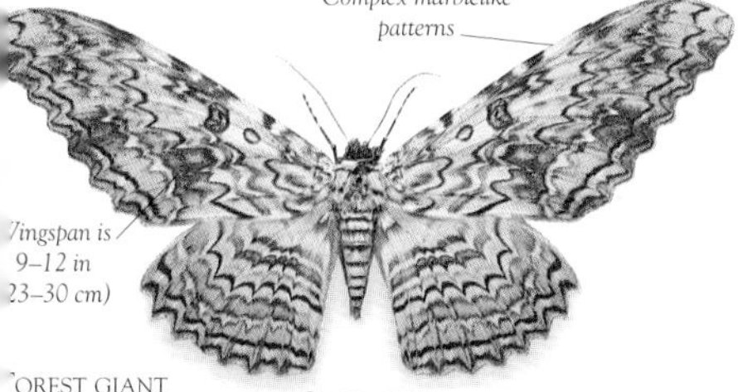

TIGER PIERID

Orange warning color

Complex marblelike patterns

Wingspan is 9–12 in (23–30 cm)

FOREST GIANT

The magnificent Giant Agrippa has the largest wingspan of any moth in the world.

GIANT AGRIPPA

QUEEN CRACKER

NOISY FLIGHT

The Queen Cracker butterfly is named after the clicking noise it makes when flying. The uppersides of the wings have iridescent blue spots. The undersides are camouflaged, making it hard to see when settled on a tree.

Blue metallic spots

Rounded hindwing

MORPHOS AND BIRDWINGS

AMONG THE BEST-KNOWN and most spectacular butterflies to flourish in the tropical rain forests are the Morphos of Central and South America and the Birdwings of Asia and Australasia. They are not related, but both have large, iridescent wings and a powerful flight. They fly through the rain forest canopy or glide along forest paths.

COMMON MORPHO

MOTHER-OF-PEARL MORPHO

PEARLY MORPHO

The delicate, translucent white Mother-of-pearl Morpho occurs only in Brazil. Both males and females have similar colors and patterns. They feed on rotting fruit, especially jackfruit. The caterpillars live in nests in forest trees.

BLUE FLASH

The intense, shimmering blues of male Morphos occur only on the uppersides of the wings. The colors help to attract females and may also serve to dazzle predators when the butterfly needs to escape. Morphos fly in zig-zags, beating their wings slowly. Each time the butterfly exposes the darke undersides of its wings, it fades into the background.

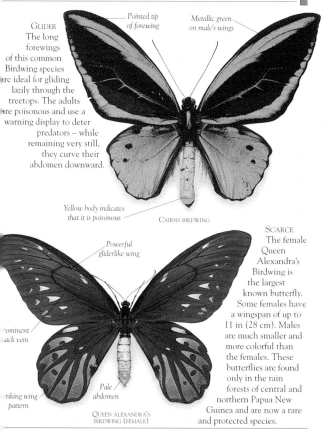

GLIDER
The long forewings of this common Birdwing species are ideal for gliding lazily through the treetops. The adults are poisonous and use a warning display to deter predators – while remaining very still, they curve their abdomen downward.

CAIRNS BIRDWING

SCARCE
The female Queen Alexandra's Birdwing is the largest known butterfly. Some females have a wingspan of up to 11 in (28 cm). Males are much smaller and more colorful than the females. These butterflies are found only in the rain forests of central and northern Papua New Guinea and are now a rare and protected species.

QUEEN ALEXANDRA'S BIRDWING (FEMALE)

TROPICAL MOTHS

TWO STRIKING FAMILIES of moths live in the tropical rain forests. The Uraniidae include colorful, day-flying species as well as pale-colored night fliers. The Brahmaeidae are active only at night. They usually have large eyespots to frighten off predators and a well-developed proboscis for feeding.

MADAGASCAN SUNSET MOTH

SUNSET COLORS
The shape and brilliant colors of this day-flying moth give it a striking resemblance to a Swallowtail butterfly. The caterpillar's habit of eating poisonous plants and the bright colors of the adult indicate that the Madagascan Sunset Moth may contain poisons. Victorians used its multicolored wings to make jewelry.

STRIPED PROTECTION
The striped wings of this small, night-flying Uraniid help to break up its outline, camouflaging the moth while it rests during the day. Its slender body is similar to those of its relatives, the Geometer moths. The *Cyphura pardata* lives only in Papua New Guinea and the neighboring islands.

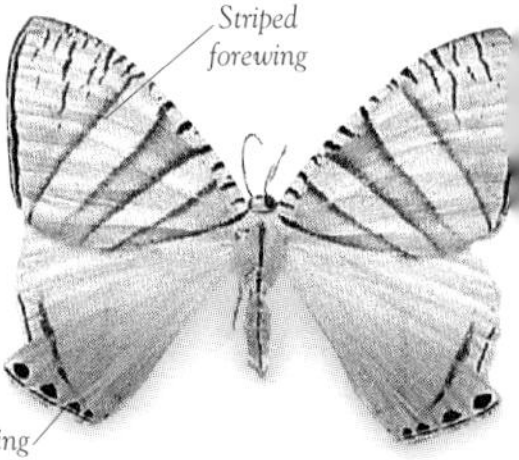

CYPHURA PARDATA

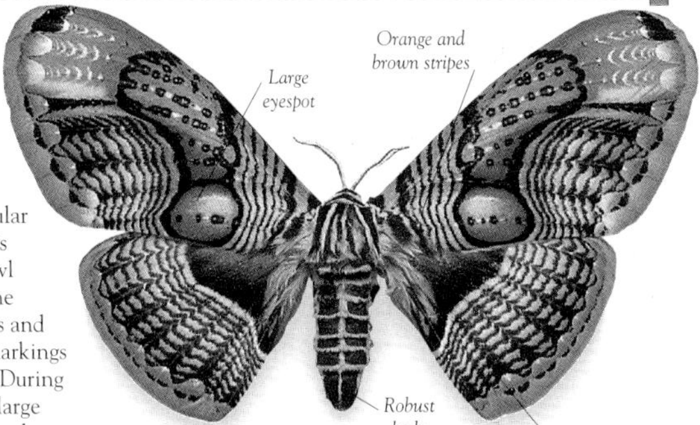

OWL MOTH

)WL EYES
'his spectacular \sian moth is alled the Owl Aoth after the irge eyespots and eatherlike markings n its wings. During he day, this large Brahmaeid moth rests on ree trunks or on the ground with its vings spread out. Although the adults ave a proboscis, they do not feed.

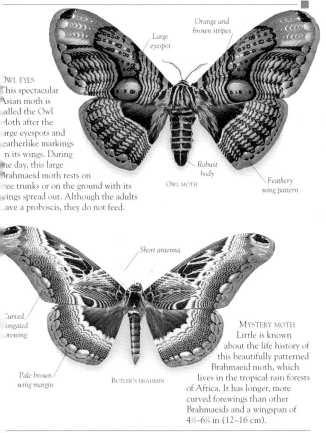

BUTLER'S BRAHMIN

MYSTERY MOTH
Little is known about the life history of this beautifully patterned Brahmaeid moth, which lives in the tropical rain forests of Africa. It has longer, more curved forewings than other Brahmaeids and a wingspan of 4½–6¼ in (12–16 cm).

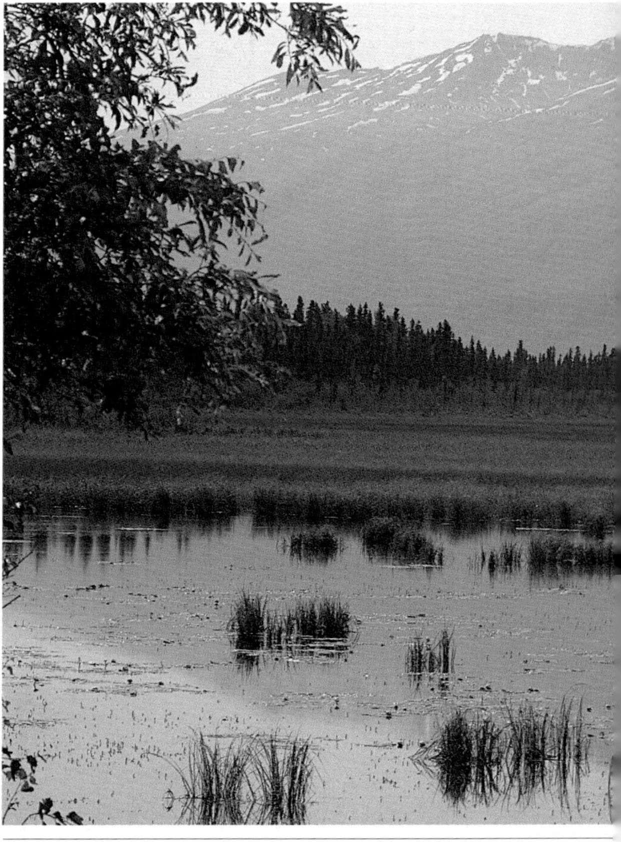

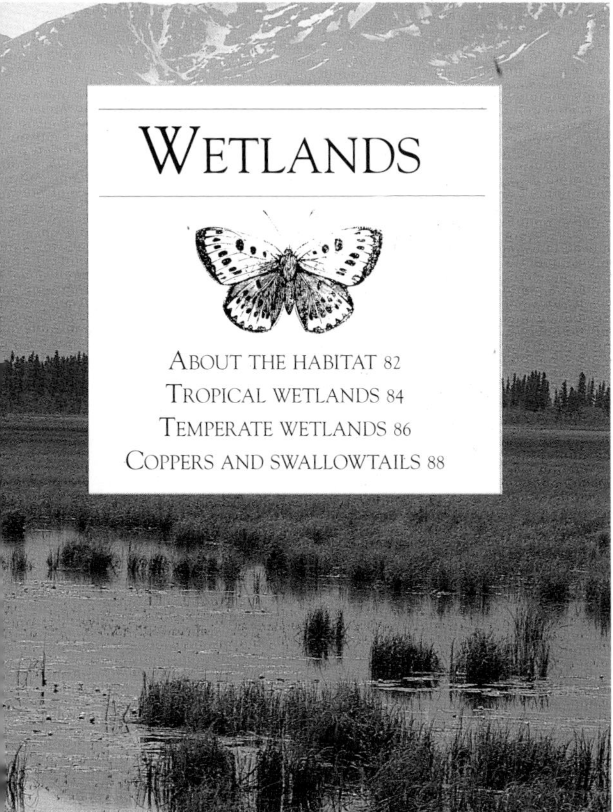

WETLANDS

ABOUT THE HABITAT

WHILE FEW BUTTERFLIES and moths live on open water some species are attracted to the plants that grow in wetland habitats. These frequently occur near rivers, lakes, and seas. Temporary wetlands, caused by seasonal flooding, are also home to some specie

WETLAND HABITATS
Six percent of the Earth's surface is covered by wetlands. These habitats occur in tropical and temperate regions and include mangrove swamps, peat bogs, and marshes.

LEAF SHELTER
The eggs of the Brown China-mark moth are laid on water plantain. When they hatch, the caterpillars mine into the leaves. Later, they use pieces of leaf to make small shelters in which to live underwater.

VICEROY
These American butterflies can often be seen by riversides, canals, lakeshores, and over marshes, flapping their wings wildly in between brief glides They lay their eggs on trees such as willow and aspen. The Viceroy is also known as the Mimic butterfly because it closely resembles the Monarch.

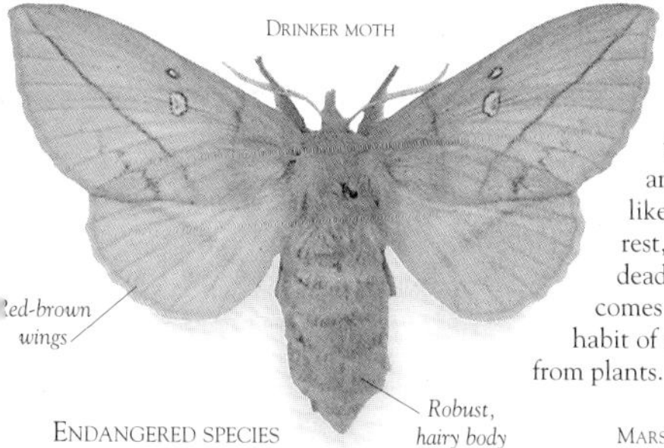

DEW DRINKER

Common in Europe and Northern Asia, Drinker moths frequent marshes, fens, and ditches, where they like to lay their eggs. At rest, the adult looks like a dead leaf. Its common name comes from the caterpillars' habit of sipping dew or raindrops from plants.

ENDANGERED SPECIES

Due to the drainage of wet meadows for agriculture, Marsh Fritillaries are rapidly declining throughout Europe and temperate Asia. They live in isolated colonies in damp meadows and on marshy hillsides, where the caterpillars' food plant, devil's-bit scabious, grows.

TROPICAL SWAMPS

The Common Eggfly butterfly lives in a wide variety of habitats from India to New Zealand, including the mangrove swamps that occur along the tropical coasts of Malaysia and Australia.

WETLAND FACTS

- The wetlands are home to a rich diversity of plant life.
- Wetlands are at risk from pollution and drainage and are disappearing rapidly all over the world.
- Tropical mangrove trees have aerial breathing roots that stick out of the water.

TROPICAL WETLANDS

THESE HOT, HUMID regions are rich in plant and animal life. However, competition for food is severe. Some butterflies and moths are able to live in tropical swamps. The caterpillars feed on mangrove trees that thrive in waterlogged soil and on aquatic plants, such as papyrus.

VARIOUS FORMS
This butterfly flourishes in the swamps of tropical North America, and in South and Central America. Many forms occur, differing in color and pattern. The spiny, silver-spotted caterpillar eats water hyssop.

UNDERWATER
The caterpillar of the South American Water Tiger moth not only lives underwater, but can swim It traps air in dense hairs that cover its body.

SEASONAL CHANGE
The Pirate Butterfly lives in the African swamps and shows seasonal changes in color. The dr season brood has dark brown win undersides, while the wet season brood has pale brown undersides.

VEAK FLIER

Che strikingly ›atterned Large Tree Nymph butterfly is widespread in southern Asia and Japan. Although a species of the forests, it ives in mangrove swamps in he southern part of its ange. In dappled sunlight, his slow-flying butterfly is lmost invisible.

WIDELY DISTRIBUTED

Tiny African Grass Blues range from southwestern Europe through Africa and Asia to Australia. They live in wetland and grassland habitats in both tropical and temperate areas. The caterpillars are green and covered with short hairs. They feed on devil's thorn.

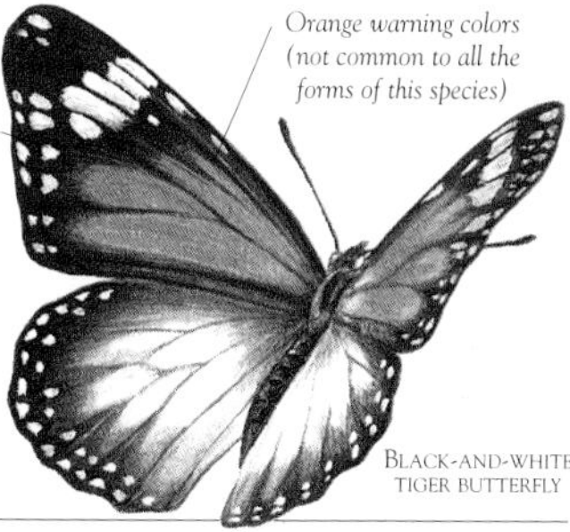

BLACK-AND-WHITE TIGER

This species lives in the mangrove swamps of Malaysia. There are many forms that live in different geographical regions from Southeast Asia to Australia. The caterpillars of the Australian form feed on poisonous milkweeds which grow in brackish (slightly salty) water.

TEMPERATE WETLANDS

MOTHS AND BUTTERFLIES are attracted to a variety of plants that grow in flat, marshy meadows. Many species flourish among reeds and bulrushes and on willow and alder trees. Only a few species can live in peat bogs, such as those in Alaska, Ireland, and New Zealand, where the plant life is largely damp mosses.

INSECT EATER
The Harvester butterfly is closely associated with alder swamps in Canada and the US. The adult butterfly drinks the honeydew produced by aphids, while the caterpillar feeds on Woolly aphids found on alder trees.

HARVESTER BUTTERFLY

LESSER MARBLED FRITILLARY

TYPICAL FRITILLARY
In much of Europe and temperate Asia, the Lesser Marbled Fritillary can be found in marshy areas where meadowsweet and great burnet grow. These are the food plants of its caterpillars. The wings of the adults have typical Fritillary markings – black spots on an orange background.

SWAMP METALMARK

ALDER

THISTLE DIET

The Swamp Metalmark, as its name implies, occurs in wet meadows and wamps in Pennsylvania, the Great ,akes, and Minnesota. The female ays eggs on the caterpillar's food lant, bog thistle.

LARGE CHECKERED SKIPPER

LARGE CHECKERED SKIPPER

This fast-flying butterfly is found n marshy meadows from southern Scandinavia to the Mediterranean. t often lives in small isolated colonies. The caterpillars feed on various grasses.

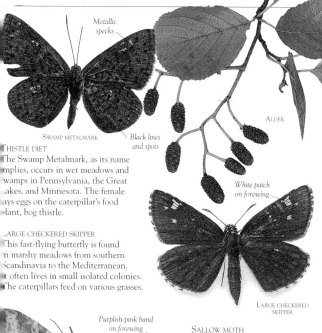

PINK-BARRED SALLOW MOTH

SALLOW MOTH

Despite its name, the brightly colored Pink-barred Sallow moth is yellow with red or purple bands on the forewings. It is widely distributed in Europe and Asia and is also found in Canada and the US. The eggs are laid on willow trees and the caterpillar feeds on willow catkins and other damp-meadow plants.

COPPERS AND SWALLOWTAILS

SOME SPECIES OF Coppers and Swallowtails live and breed in wetland habitats. Coppers are small, swift fliers – their iridescent wings flash in the sun. The large Swallowtail butterflies can also be brightly colored and tend to have a slow, flapping flight.

Duller colors of female

LARGE COPPER FEMALE

Brighter colors of male

LARGE COPPER MALE

Purple patches

PURPLE-EDGED COPPER

MAGNIFICENT MALES

In common with other members of the Lycaenidae, male and female Coppers are often different colors. The males of the Large Copper, which lives in wet meadows and marshes, are a much brighter orange-red than the duller females. The caterpillars feed on dock plants, especially water dock.

HABITAT THREAT

Both the Purple-edged Copper and the Large Copper have declined in number, their marshy habitats have been drained for cultivation. They hibernate as young caterpillars and resume feeding in spring

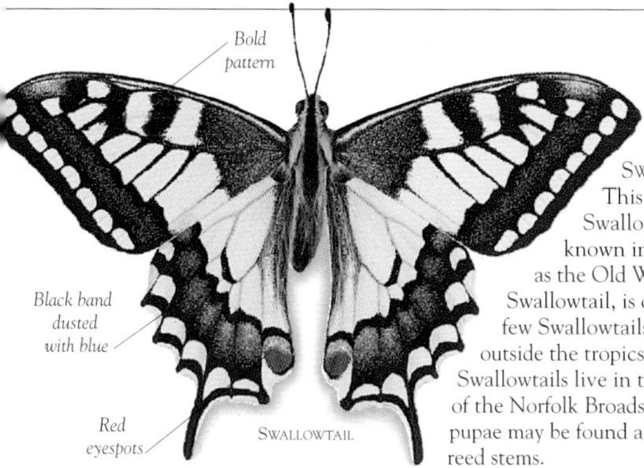

SWALLOWTAIL

This species of Swallowtail, known in the US as the Old World Swallowtail, is one of the few Swallowtails to occur outside the tropics. In Britain, Swallowtails live in the reed beds of the Norfolk Broads; their pupae may be found attached to reed stems.

KITE BUTTERFLY

The Zebra Swallowtail is the most common of the Kite Swallowtails, named after their triangular wings and long tails. Zebra Swallowtails live in moist, shaded, lowland woods. There are several generations a year; the adults that emerge in spring have shorter tails and are smaller and whiter than the later broods.

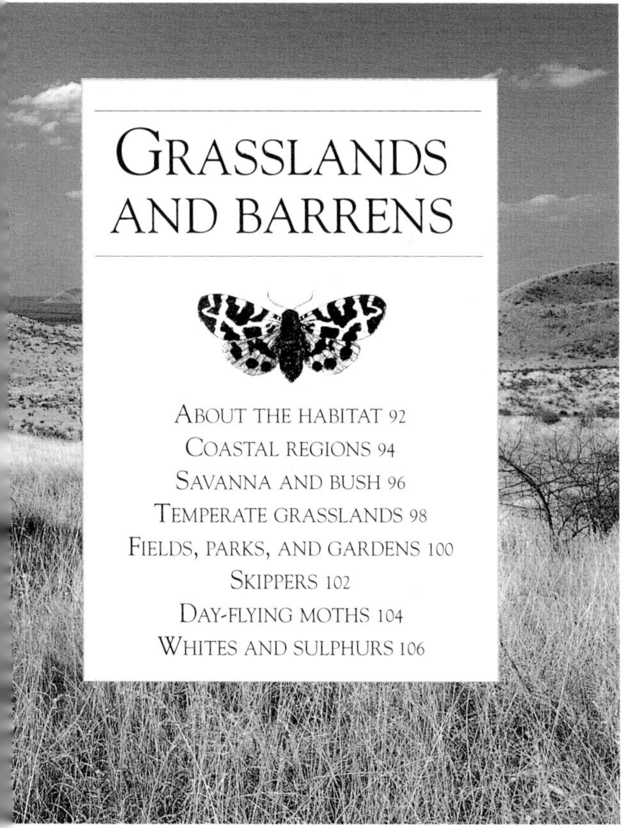

GRASSLANDS AND BARRENS

About the Habitat

GRASSY HABITATS ARE important breeding grounds. There are plenty of grasses on which the caterpillars can feed and many flowers to attract butterflies and moths. On windy days, they find it hard to fly in open grasslands and shelter low down among the grasses.

IN THE LONG GRASS
Brown butterflies, such as this Meadow Brown, prefer medium to tall grass. Their caterpillars hide deep in grass clumps by day and climb up the stems to eat the juicy tips after dark.

HEATHLAND BUTTERFLIES
Blues, such as the Silver-Studded Blue, frequent low-growing grasslands and heathlands. Most heaths have poor soils and are dominated by heather plants; grasses grow in the wetter areas.

GARDEN VISITOR
Although brightly colored, the Garden Tiger moth flies mainly at night. As its common name suggests, it frequents gardens, where the female lays her eggs on a wide variety of plants.

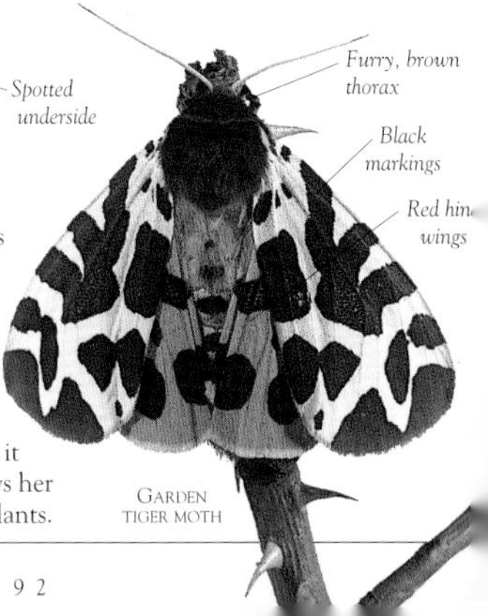

BUCKEYE BUTTERFLY

HORELINE VISITORS

autumn, hordes of Buckeyes migrate southward ong the east coast of the United States. They live nd breed in open fields and scrubland. The adults ibernate during the winter.

GRASSLAND FACTS

- Farming and building projects threaten areas of grassland and barrens.
- Agricultural fields do not contain the right species of plants for many species to survive.
- Grassland species include Browns, Blues, Skippers, Burnets, and Grass moths.

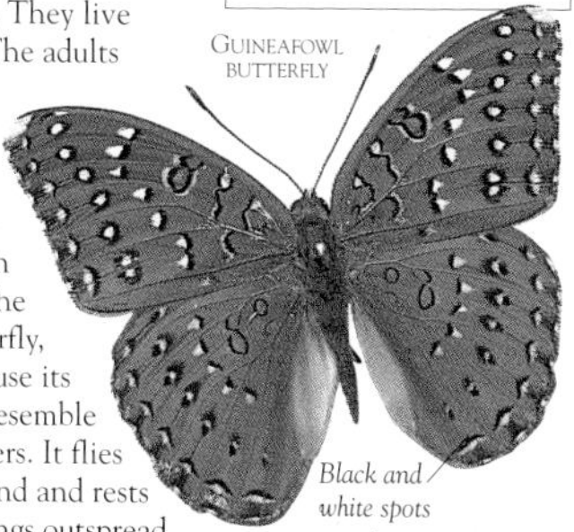

GUINEAFOWL BUTTERFLY

AFRICAN SCRUBLAND

A common sight in the African bush is the Guineafowl butterfly, so called because its spotted wings resemble Guineafowl feathers. It flies close to the ground and rests with its wings outspread.

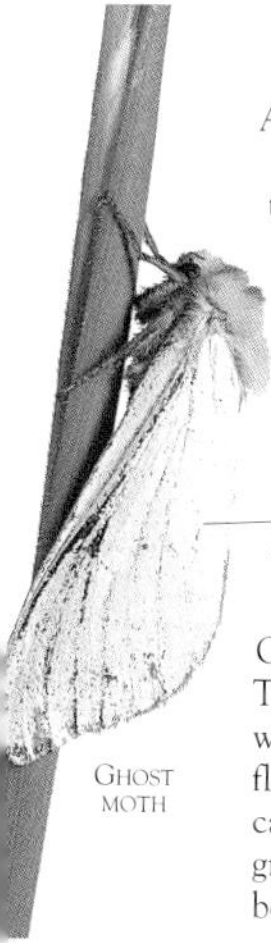

GHOST MOTH

GHOSTLY PEST

The male Ghost moth's shiny white wings attract females as he flies over meadows at dusk. The caterpillars feed on the roots of grasses and other plants and can become agricultural pests.

Butterflies are attracted to broad flowers, like this dandelion.

COASTAL REGIONS

SAND DUNES, GRASSLANDS, and barrens near the coas provide favorable habitats for butterflies and moths, especially in sheltered locations where wild herbs anc flowers grow. Building, tourism, and intensive farmin along coasts has reduced the diversity of species.

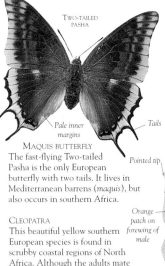

MAQUIS BUTTERFLY
The fast-flying Two-tailed Pasha is the only European butterfly with two tails. It lives in Mediterranean barrens (*maquis*), but also occurs in southern Africa.

TAILLESS SWALLOWTAIL
The Spanish Festoon is a Swallowtail without the long tails typical of its relatives. It flies from February to May among the rough, dry barrens of the hilly Mediterranean coast of southwest Europe.

CLEOPATRA
This beautiful yellow southern European species is found in scrubby coastal regions of North Africa. Although the adults mate before hibernating, the females do not lay their eggs until the spring.

STRIPED CATERPILLARS

Mainly found on the Australian coasts of Queensland and Victoria, the Painted Skipper can also be seen in the Blue Mountains in New South Wales. The caterpillars have striped bodies to camouflage them among the sword grasses on which they live.

POISONOUS BODY

White Ermine moths inhabit coastal dunes in Europe, Asia, and Japan. Their colorful, poisonous abdomens stand out against their white wings. The hairy caterpillars can move at high speed.

DUNE GEM

Common Opal butterflies live among the sand dunes of southern Africa. The male can be distinguished from the female by the extensive blue patches on his copper wings.

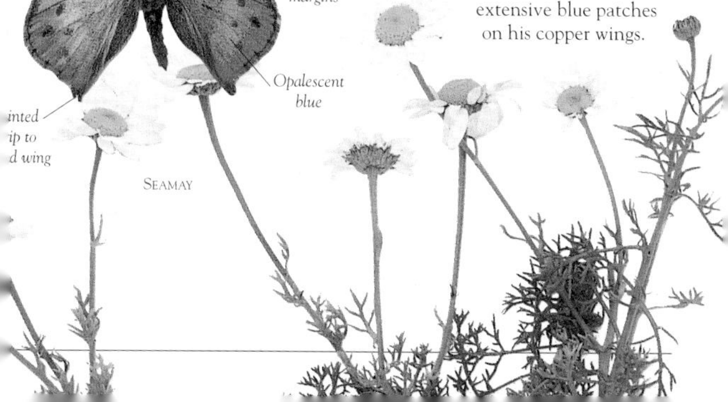

SAVANNA AND BUSH

THE BUTTERFLIES AND MOTHS of the African savanna, Australian bush, and Asian scrub have to survive dry seasons, or follow the rain to where plants are plentiful. Larvae and pupae often remain dormant during the hot summer.

PALM SKIPPER

DATE AT DUSK

When dusk comes to the Afric savanna, Palm Skippers witl their distinctive white wing spots, fly near phoenix date palms on which their caterpillars feed.

EUCALYPTUS

BLUE PANSY (MALE)

BLUE PANSY

This butterfly can be seer flitting about in hot sunshine in a variety of habitats, including bush areas in Africa, Australia, and Asia.

BANKSIA MOTH

DEFENSE

The spotted caterpillar of the Australian Banksia Moth feeds during the day on the leaves of banksia and hakea plants. If disturbed, the front part of its body rears up.

DARK CHOPPER MOTH

IRRITATING HAIR

Caterpillars of the Dark Chopper feed on acacia and other plants of the African savanna. Their bodies are covered with hairs that can irritate human skin. This moth gets its name from the male's sharply angled hind wings.

LARGE BLUE CHARAXES

STRONG WINGS

Powerful fliers from the tropical African scrub, Large Blue Charaxes feed on rotten fruit or tree sap. The males also visit patches of mud to absorb nutrients. The caterpillars are reen and feed on pod mahogany trees.

YELLOW COSTER

AD TASTE

edators find e caterpillars of the ellow Coster from uthern Asia doubly disgusting. They ed on poisonous plants, giving them a d taste, and they also give off a foul nell. They assemble in groups to aximize the stink.

ACACIA

TEMPERATE GRASSLANDS

WITH THEIR MANY kinds of wildflowers and grasses, temperate grasslands are ideal habitats. Warm, south-facing chalk and limestone slopes are home to a particularly rich variety of moths and butterflies.

CHECKERED WINGS
A member of the Browns, the Marbled White butterfly feeds on flowers such as thistles. Early and late in the day, it may be seen resting on grassheads, holding its checkered wings open.

SUNBATHER
The Wall or Wall Brown is named after its habit of basking on sunny walls, short grass, and bare soil. With its wings closed, it blends well with the bare ground.

SPRING BUTTERFLIES
Orange Tips are found in Europe and Asia. Both sexes show the mottled green undersides of their wings as they drink from spring flowers.

BEAUTIFUL BLUE

Widespread throughout Europe, the Adonis Blue is named after the handsome boy loved by the Greek goddess, Aphrodite. It lives in colonies on chalk and limestone grasslands and :eeds on wildflowers. Males often gather to feed on animal droppings.

INTRUDERS BEWARE!

One of the most common species in the northern hemisphere, the Small Copper is often found near flowers, basking in the sun with its wings open. Males are apt to chase away other butterflies that intrude into their territory. The camouflaged caterpillars feed on dock leaves.

:HALK GRASSLANDS

'he Silver-spotted Skipper can be :en on grazed, chalk grasslands . Europe. The caterpillar ves in a rolled-up leaf iade and forms a cocoon om grass and soil.

FIELDS, PARKS, AND GARDENS

A WIDE RANGE of butterflies and moths visits these man-made habitats, which often contain plants that also grow in natural grasslands. They provide useful feeding stations for passing moths and butterflies.

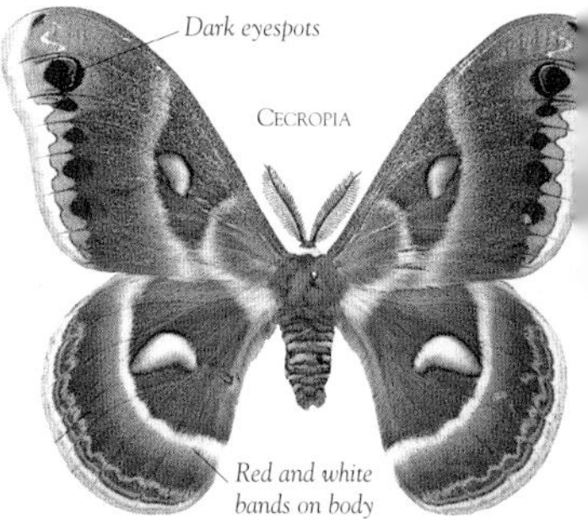

GARDEN GIANT
Found from March to June in fields and gardens in the US and southern Canada, the *Cecropia* (commonly called the Robin Moth because of its red body) is the largest North American moth.

UNWELCOME GUEST
Christmas in South Africa often brings the Citrus Swallowtail, also called the Christmas butterfly. However, its arrival is not welcomed by fruit growers since its caterpillars are highly destructive pests of citrus trees.

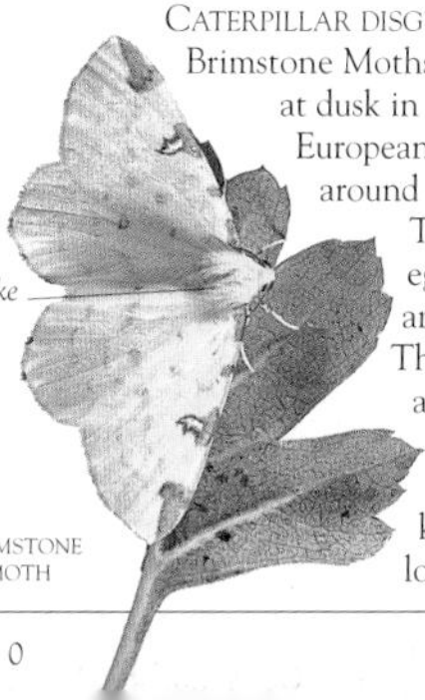

CATERPILLAR DISGUISE
Brimstone Moths can be seen at dusk in northern European gardens and around hedgerows. They lay their eggs on hawtho and blackthorn. The caterpillars are very well camouflaged when they keep still, they look like twigs.

CABBAGE WHITES

Large Whites, also known as Cabbage Whites, are common in vegetable gardens and cabbage fields in Europe. They lay their eggs on cabbage or nasturtium plants. The pupae overwinter in sheltered spots and the adults emerge in April.

Black wing tips
LARGE WHITE

rdy legs
e spurs
k and olive-
wn stripes
ELEPHANT HAWKMOTH

ROBUST HAWKMOTH

Across Europe and Asia, the Elephant Hawkmoth may be seen speeding from flower to flower at dusk. Its long tongue probes into deep-throated flowers. In gardens and parks the large caterpillars feed on fuchsia.

SMALL TORTOISESHELL

Points on
edges of
forewing
and
hind wing

ARDEN BUTTERFLY

e Small Tortoiseshell is mmon in European gardens, d can be seen resting on wers or near patches of nettles, which it lays its eggs. The dersides of its wings are nouflaged to look like tree bark.

e plants attract a
wide variety of
butterflies.

SKIPPERS

SUNNY, TROPICAL, AND TEMPERATE grasslands are hon to about 3,000 species of mothlike butterflies known as Skippers. Their common name comes from the wa they busily skip from flower to flower. Most are small with dull brown or orange-brown coloring. Their caterpillars usually feed on grasses, living and pupatii inside rolled-up leaves, drawn together with silk.

SKIPPER SHAPE
A typical Skipper has a large head, thick body, and short, triangular-shaped forewings. The antennae, which are widely separated at the base, usually have swollen or curved tips that end with a point. Skipper caterpillars have a large head, a thin neck, and a body that tapers at each end.

GRIZZLED SKIPPER

DINGY SKIPPER

LAZY SUNBATHERS
Dingy Skippers live in small colonies on grassy hills and open heaths in Europe and Asia. They spend long periods basking in the sunshine, with th wings held open. At night, or in cold weather, they rest on the tops of grasses draping their wings around the stems.

SILK SPINNERS

Large Skippers spend much of their time establishing territorial bases. The caterpillars shelter, hibernate, and pupate inside a tube made of grass blades, wrapped with cords of silk.

LARGE SKIPPER

GIANT YUCCA SKIPPER

YUCCA SKIPPERS

These large skippers with stout abdomens are found only in southern parts of the US and Central America. They differ from other skippers in that they have smaller heads and antennae that are set relatively close at the base.

LONG-TAILED SKIPPER

LONG-TAILS

The hind wings of some Skippers in the Americas are elongated into long tails, not unlike those of the Swallowtail butterflies. The Long-tailed Skipper can be distinguished from other Long-tails in North America by the iridescent green-blue on the upperside of the wings. The larva feeds on wild and cultivated beans and is known as the "Bean Leaf Roller" or the "Roller Worm."

DAY-FLYING MOTHS

OFTEN MISTAKEN FOR BUTTERFLIES, colorful day-flying moths abound in summer meadows and pastures. Many have conspicuous warning colors to tell predators that they are poisonous or that they taste unpleasant. As they fly from flower to flower seeking nectar to drink, some day fliers bear a striking resemblance to bees and wasps.

POISONOUS PLANTS

Striking Cinnabar Moths obtain their poisons from the caterpillar's food plant. Large numbers of this species' orange and black caterpillars are often seen feeding on poisonous ragwort plants. When ready to pupate, they burrow underground.

CINNABAR MOTH

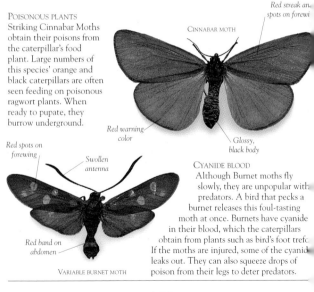

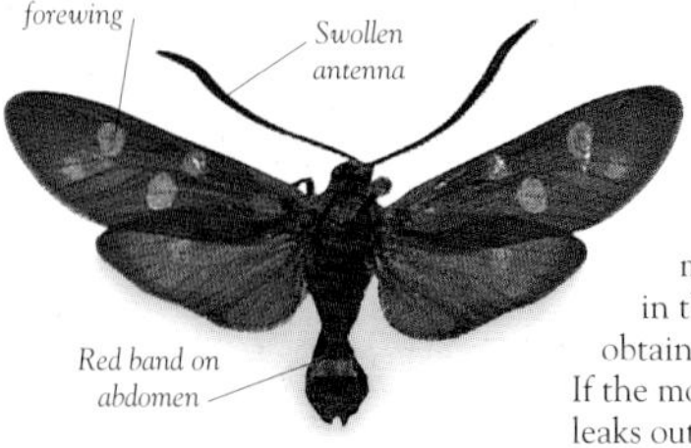

VARIABLE BURNET MOTH

CYANIDE BLOOD

Although Burnet moths fly slowly, they are unpopular with predators. A bird that pecks a burnet releases this foul-tasting moth at once. Burnets have cyanide in their blood, which the caterpillars obtain from plants such as bird's foot trefc If the moths are injured, some of the cyanid leaks out. They can also squeeze drops of poison from their legs to deter predators.

TIGER MOTHS
Some colorful Tiger moths synthesize their own poisons. Their caterpillars feed on a variety of harmless plants, and are protected by unappetizing hairs rather than by poisons. The larvae are commonly known as "Woolly Bears."

SCARLET TIGER

BIRD OR MOTH?
The hum of its rapidly beating wings and its darting flight give the Hummingbird Hawkmoth its remarkable resemblance to a hummingbird. These tiny moths hover in front of flowers, sucking up nectar with a long proboscis.

HUMMINGBIRD HAWKMOTH

BEE MIMIC
With its clear wings and furry body, the King's Bee Hawkmoth resembles a bee. When the moth emerges from its pupa, its wings are completely covered with scales, but these fall off when it flies. Quickly darting from flower to flower, these moths also behave like bees.

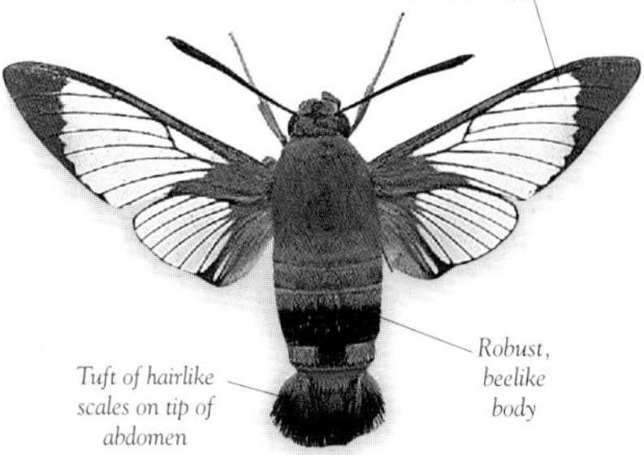

KING'S BEE HAWKMOTH

WHITES AND SULPHURS

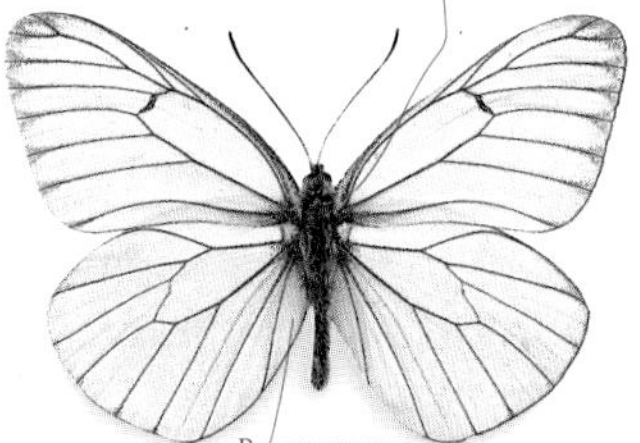

BLACK-VEINED WHITE

THESE BUTTERFLIES are found in open, sunny places where their caterpillars' food plants grow. The markings and colors of Whites and Sulphurs may vary during the year, being darker in summer.

DECLINING NUMBERS
The Black-veined White used to be common across Europe and temperate Asia in orchards and hedgerows. It has declined in number in some areas. The caterpillars hibernate in a communal silk nest.

CABBAGE BUTTERFLY

SMALL BUT WIDE-RANGING
Often seen fluttering in gardens across the Northern hemisphere and also in Australia, the Cabbage Butterfly is one of the most widely distributed butterflies. Its caterpillars damage cabbages and some garden flowers.

BATH WHITE

SUMMER VISITOR
A regular summer migrant from southern Europe and North Africa to many parts of northern Europe, the Bath White prefers warm, dry grasslands. Although a rare visitor to Britain, it is named after the city in southwestern England. The undersides of its wings have olive-green markings.

ORANGE SPOTS
Caterpillars of the Orange Sulphur are pests of the alfalfa crop and also feed on clovers. The species is common in many parts of the US and Mexico. The color of the adults varies, but they always have an orange spot on their hind wings, which distinguishes them from the Common Sulphur.

ORANGE SULPHUR

Orange spot

CLOUDLESS SULPHUR

Black spotting at wing edge

ONE-WAY TRAVELER
In summer, the Cloudless Sulphur migrates northward from Mexico and the southern US. Large and fast-flying, it covers great distances, traveling around the Caribbean or up to New York. The migrants do not live long enough to return south. The reason for this mass migration is unknown.

Brown markings

Orange wing tip

Fast, powerful fliers

GREAT ORANGE TIP

SECRETIVE FEMALES
There are usually two generations a year of Great Orange Tip butterflies; the wet season brood tends to be larger than the dry season generation. While the males prefer open country, the females live mainly in the forests. When they rest on the ground, they mimic dead leaves.

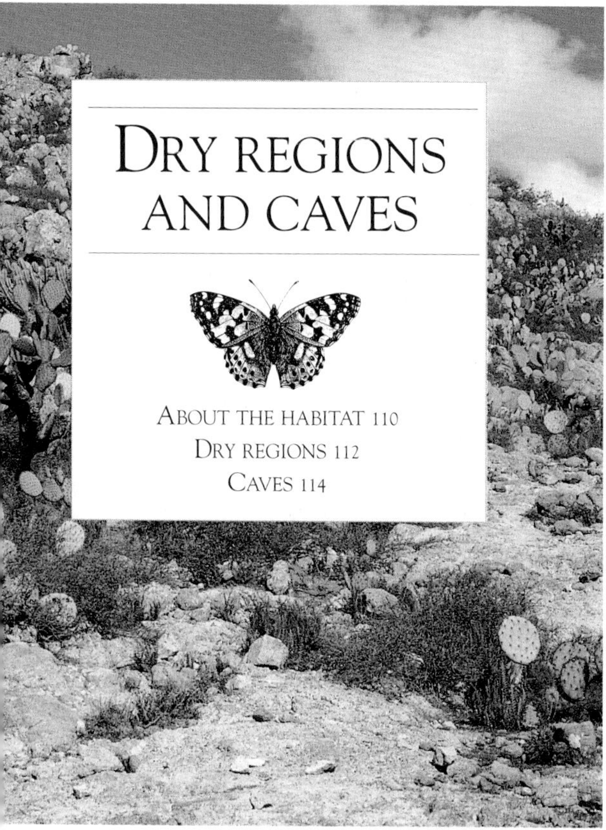

DRY REGIONS AND CAVES

ABOUT THE HABITAT

DRY REGIONS ARE characterized by low rainfall, extreme temperatures, and sparse vegetation. Only hardy moths and butterflies can survive such hostile environments. Some species seek refuge in damp, dark caves, where the temperature remains constant throughout the year.

TIGER BL
The Little Tig
Blue butterfly li
in hot, dry regions
the Near and Middle Ea
The caterpillars feed on t
jujube bush – a small, tough, sp
shrub, also known as Christ's tho

AFRICAN RINGLET
Widespread throughout Africa, south of the Sahara, and southwest Asia, the African Ringlet has an eye-catching, bouncing flight.

PEACOCK BUTTERFLY

Camouflaged undersides

PEACOCK

For some moths and butterflies, caves provide shelter from harsh weather conditions. The Peacock butterfly hibernates as an adult in caves during the cold, northern winter. The dark undersides of its wings help to camouflage it from predators such as birds.

/ITCHETTY GRUBS

ɜveral species of ustralian ghost oth larvae feed on .e roots of plants in id regions. The large .terpillars, known as /itchetty grubs, are .ten by some boriginal peoples.

Green foreleg

This is one of the Ghost moths that produce Witchetty grubs

SPLENDID GHOST MOTH

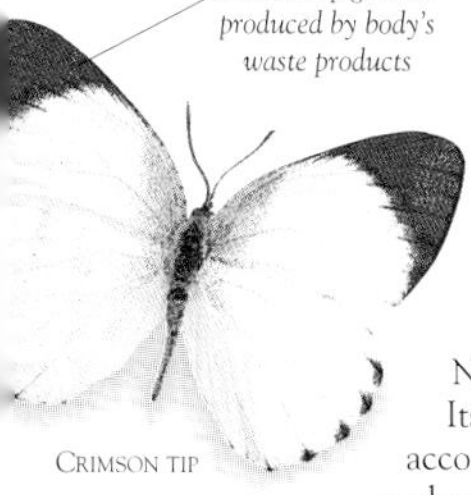

Crimson pigments produced by body's waste products

CRIMSON TIP

VARIATIONS

The Crimson Tip butterfly is found in arid, thornbush land in Africa, the Near East, and India. Its appearance varies according to the season and region.

DESERT FACTS

- To prevent water loss, plants in semideserts have small leaves.
- Oases in deserts are a vital lifeline for animal life.
- Overgrazing can turn dry grasslands into deserts.

DRY REGIONS

VAST AREAS OF SEMIDESERT occur on most continents. The hot, dry days can lead to rapid water loss and death for many butterflies and moths. Many species migrate in search of rain. Others survive by feeding on tough, thorny desert plants that store water in their stems to protec against drought.

YUCCA SKIPPERS
Yucca Skipper butterflies of Central and South America do not feed as adults, although related species sometimes drink from moist ground. Their caterpillars bore into the fleshy stems, leaves, or roots of yuccas and agaves.

LANG'S SHORT-TAILED BLUE
This butterfly lives in a variety of habitat southern Europe and the Middle East. It adapts to dry climates and is often seen fluttering in dry Mediterranean sc

BENT-WING GHOST MOTH

DESERT GHOST
The large Australia Bent-wing Ghos moth sometime leaves its forest habitat, and can be spotted shimmering across the desert at dusk.

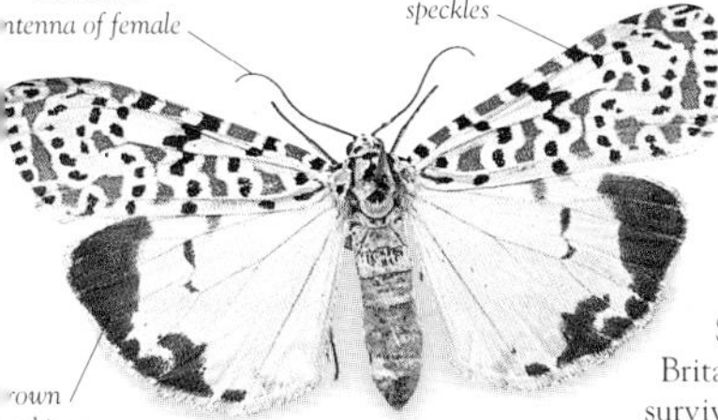

CRIMSON SPECKLED MOTH

MIGRATION

Crimson Speckled Moths occur in Africa, southern Europe, and the Middle East. In desert areas, they gravitate toward oases. This is a migratory species and occasionally Crimson Speckled Moths have reached Britain. However, they cannot survive the cold, northern winter.

WHITE-LINED SPHINX

CACTUS

IDE RANGE

ıe powerful, fast-flying White-ıed Sphinx can survive in dry eas, but like many other gratory species, it occurs in a de variety of habitats throughout orth and South America, Europe, rica, Asia, and Australia. It ooth a day- and night-ing species.

CAVES

THE TEMPERATURE IN caves remains almost constant throughout the year. In harsh environments, caves are ideal places for moths and butterflies to hibernate or estivate (lie dormant during hot, dry summer months). Some small moths spend their entire lives in caves, feeding on the droppings of bats and other animals.

Colors blend with rocks

ALPINE CAVES
In spring, Bogong Moths gather in caves and rock crevices in the Australian Alps. They remain dormant during the hot, dry summer. Their gray-brown coloring helps to conceal them from predators.

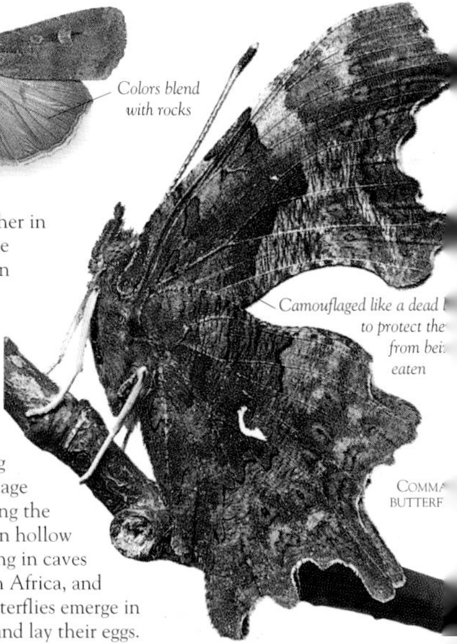

Camouflaged like a dead l to protect the from bei eaten

COMMA BUTTERF

CAMOUFLAGE
Comma butterflies are characterized by ragged wing margins that help to camouflage them. They hibernate during the winter, sometimes roosting in hollow tree trunks or hiding in caves throughout Europe, North Africa, and temperate Asia. The butterflies emerge in the spring to mate and lay their eggs.

HERALD MOTH

This widespread moth ranges from Canada and the US, across Europe to Japan. The caterpillar feeds on willow, and the adult uses small barbs on its proboscis to pierce fruit. During the northern winter, the adults hibernate in caves.

COMMON BROWN BUTTERFLY

SURVIVING THE HEAT

After mating, the male of this Australian butterfly dies in the summer heat. However, the female Common Brown flies off to find shelter, sometimes in the entrances of caves. She estivates over the summer and reemerges later in the year to produce another generation.

OLD LADY MOTH

DAYTIME RETREAT

The night-flying Old Lady Moth is known in Europe for its habit of creeping behind shutters and curtains or hiding in sheds or caves during daylight hours.

Arctic and Mountains

ABOUT THE HABITAT

IN THE SEVERE CLIMATES of Arctic and mountain habitats, there ar fierce winds, intensely cold winters, and very short summers. Moths and butterflies have adapted for survival against the elements. Many fly only when the air is still, making short, low flights from one shelter to another.

ANTIFREEZE
Many Arctic species, such as this Arctic Clouded Yellow butterfly, have a type of "antifreeze" in their blood to help them survive freezing temperatures.

MOUNTAIN AND ARCTIC

- Some butterflies live at altitudes of over 16,400 ft (5,000 m).
- Caterpillars of some Arctic and mountain species can take over three years to mature.
- Some pupae may be frozen and thawed several times.

ANTLER MOTH
Named after the antlerlike markings on the forewings, the Antler Moth flies by day and at night. It occurs in Asia, Siberia, and North America on upland moors at altitudes up to 6,560 ft (2,000 m).

ANTLER MOTH

THE HERMIT

THE HERMIT BUTTERFLY
The mottled coloring of the Hermit helps to camouflage it on the bare, rocky mountainsides of Europe. The caterpillar feeds mainly on blue moor grass and hibernates during the winter.

PIEDMONT RINGLET

RINGLET
The dark colors of the Piedmont Ringlet help this butterfly absorb as much sunshine as possible. In June and July, it flies over the stony, grassy slopes of mountains in southern Europe at 5,000–6,000 ft (1,520–1,830 m) above sea level.

COMMON WALL BUTTERFLY

OW FLIER
he Common Wall butterfly of Iran, dia, and western China lives on nny mountainsides above 6,560 ft ,000 m). To avoid being blown by inds, it flies close to the ground.

NOW YOU SEE IT
The Silver butterfly inhabits high mountain areas of the Andes. Its silvery wings are reflective, making ne butterfly shine brightly and then seemingly disappear.

SILVER BUTTERFLY

ARCTIC AND TUNDRA

DURING THE BRIEF Arctic summer, the snow melts and flowers bloom on the windswept, treeless tundra. A few hardy species of butterflies and moths emerge to take advantage of the long days and feed on the flowers. Many Arctic species are small and hairy.

WOOLLY COAT
This caterpillar sometime basks in the sun. The dar colors of the "Woolly Bear" caterpillar help to absorb the weak northerr sunshine. Its long, hairy coat traps body warmth.

ICE EDGE
The Arctic Fritillary live in tundra from the US across northern Europe t Asia, and has been foun farther north than any other species of fritillary. is one of only about six species of butterfly to survive in Greenland, whe it lives on strips of greenery that skirt a thick layer of ice.

Color variation

The Northern Clouded Yellow is distributed across the Arctic circle. It can be seen flitting low across grassy tussocks from late June to August. Due to the cold climate, it may take two years for the caterpillar to mature. The male is orange-yellow on the upperside, while the female is a dusky grayish yellow with spots between the dark veins.

Eyespot on underside
This quick-flying butterfly takes a rest

Northern clouded yellow

Rock or moth?

Well-camouflaged against a rocky background, the *Gynaephora rossii* moth keeps still to avoid being detected by day. The adult moth cannot feed and lives on the food eaten and stored during its life as a caterpillar. Both adults and caterpillars are covered with hairs to give extra warmth.

Arctic wormwood
Grows on rocky ridges and gravel banks throughout the Arctic
Gynaephora rossii
Resting with wings covering body
Lichen-encrusted, Arctic rocks

MOUNTAIN MOORLANDS

MOORLANDS cover mountainsides with a blanket of low-growing plants, including moss, heather, coarse grass, and bilberry. Weather conditions out on the moors are often very cold, wet, and windy, but several species of moths and butterflies have adapted to this harsh environment and can survive the long winters.

THREATENED SPECIES
Once widespread on upland moors in Europe and North America, the Moorland Clouded Yellow has declined in number. Its habitats are threatened by the spread of agricultural land and conifer plantations.

MOORLAND BOUNCER
The dark brown Dryad butterfly bounces as it flies over moorland meadows in Europe and temperate Asia. The female lays her eggs on grasses, such as purple moor grass. The caterpillars feed at night and hibernate in the winter.

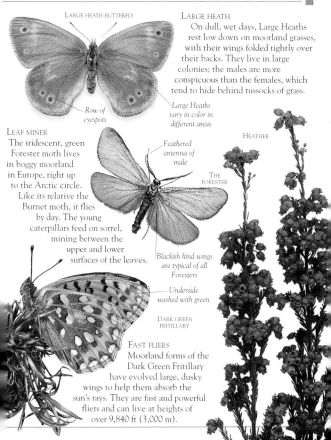

LARGE HEATH BUTTERFLY

LARGE HEATH

On dull, wet days, Large Heaths rest low down on moorland grasses, with their wings folded tightly over their backs. They live in large colonies; the males are more conspicuous than the females, which tend to hide behind tussocks of grass.

LEAF MINER

The iridescent, green Forester moth lives in boggy moorland in Europe, right up to the Arctic circle. Like its relative the Burnet moth, it flies by day. The young caterpillars feed on sorrel, mining between the upper and lower surfaces of the leaves.

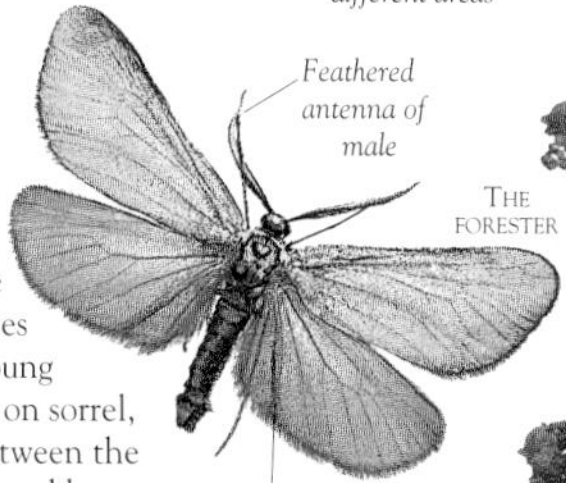

THE FORESTER

HEATHER

DARK GREEN FRITILLARY

FAST FLIERS

Moorland forms of the Dark Green Fritillary have evolved large, dusky wings to help them absorb the sun's rays. They are fast and powerful fliers and can live at heights of over 9,840 ft (3,000 m).

MOUNTAIN FORESTS

THE VEGETATION growing on mountainsides changes with the altitude. Warmer, deciduous forests on the lower slopes give way to cooler, coniferous forests higher up. These different forest habitats are home to a fascinating variety of butterflies and moths, including some of the most spectacular *Lepidoptera* in the world.

SPRUCE CONES
Typical of mountain forests are evergreen coniferous trees, such as pines, spruces, and firs.

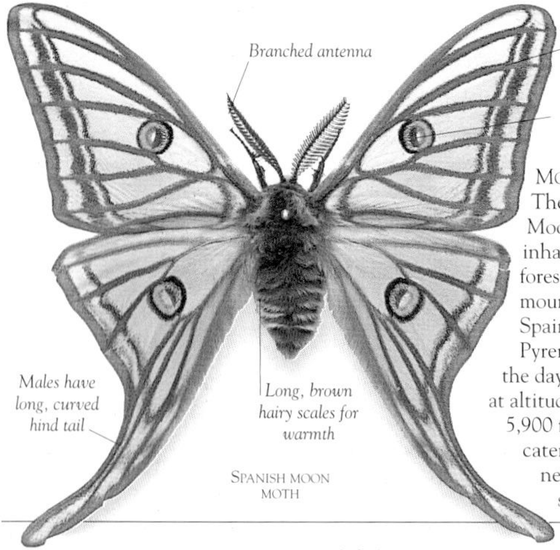

SPANISH MOON MOTH

MOON MOTH
The beautiful Spanish Moon Moth is an inhabitant of pine forests in the mountains of central Spain and the Pyrenees. It flies during the day and also at night at altitudes of up to 5,900 ft (1,800 m). The caterpillar eats the needles of various species of pine.

When resting,
luller forewings
conceal hind
wings
If alarmed, the
Bhutan Glory
flashes eyespots
Tails to distract
predator

BHUTAN GLORY

ARE GLORY

ıdly, it is now a
re sight to see the beautiful
ıutan Glory flying among the
wer forests of mountains
India and Thailand.
ıis butterfly has long
een a collector's prize.

Orange band
Sharp point on
forewing
White band
on hind
wing

BICOLOR COMMODORE

FOREST DWELLER

The Bicolor Commodore Butterfly is quite common in the forests of India, Pakistan, and Burma. In July and August, it flies up to altitudes of 8,000 ft (2,440 m) through the mountain forests. Males and females look alike.

Metallic gold-
green of male
Silver Hairstreak
Tiny tail

HIGH FLIER

This iridescent butterfly reaches altitudes of between 5,900–9,840 ft (1,800–3,000 m) in the Himalayas. Its common name, Silver Hairstreak, comes from the silvery undersides of its wings. The caterpillars feed on oak leaves.

ALPINE MEADOWS

GRASSY MEADOWS OCCUR above the tree line on mountain slopes. It is cold and windy and the soils are too thin for trees or bushes to survive. However, when the snows melt, an abundance of wildflowers an grasses attract butterflies and moths. Since summers are short, species tend to breed only once a year.

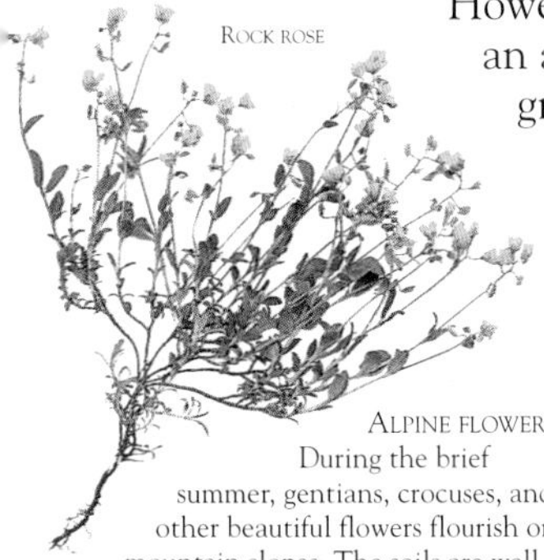

ROCK ROSE

ALPINE FLOWERS
During the brief summer, gentians, crocuses, and other beautiful flowers flourish on mountain slopes. The soils are well watered, since they are covered in snow for over half the year.

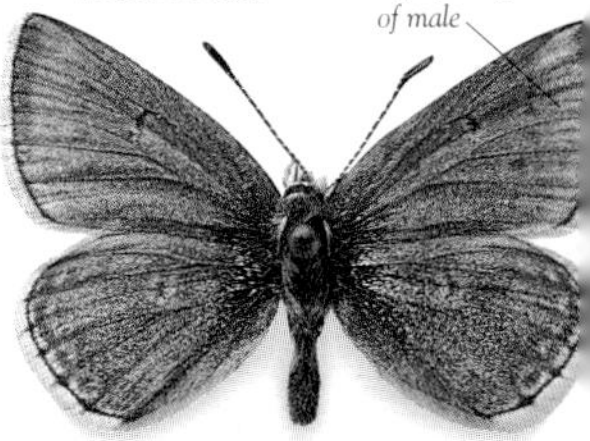

HIGH MOUNTAIN BLUE

SLOW DEVELOPERS
The eggs of the High Mountain Blue n be found on rock-jasmine. The caterpil feeds on alpine plants and develops mo slowly than its lowland relatives.

ALPINE SKIPPER

ALPINE SKIPPER
This Skipper is found in the mountains southeast Australia. The adults are on th wing in February and March, and often fee on yellow flowers of the daisy family.

ʼYNTHIA'S FRITILLARY

ʼynthia's Fritillary flies swiftly when ɔt feeding on meadow flowers. It lives nly in the European Alps and the .ountains of Bulgaria. Since there are ıany similar-looking Fritillary species, ɔth females and males use their scented heromones to identify and attract a mate.

CYNTHIA'S FRITILLARY

Yellow, black, and orange checkered wing markings

Network of veins outlined by darker scales

PEAK WHITE BUTTERFLY

CLOSE RELATIVES

The Peak White butterfly of Europe and Asia is closely related to the Western White found in the mountains of the US. It is well adapted to living at altitudes of over 6,000 ft (1,830 m) and can be found in sunny mountain habitats.

ʼARNING SIGNALS

ıis striking Ruby Tiger moth can be found the mountains of Europe, Japan, Canada, and the US at altitudes of up to 9,840 ft (3,000 m). The red and black abdomen and red wings warn predators of its disgusting taste.

Translucent, brown-red forewings

Red and black markings indicate internal poisons

ʼBY TIGER MOTH

MOUNTAIN AVENS

BLUES

SMALL, SWIFT-FLYING Blues are able to cope with mountain winds and are a common sight in alpine meadows. The males, with their glittering metallic colors, are usually more conspicuous than the females, which often have little or no blue on their wings. The caterpillars of some species live in close association with ants.

ALPINE ARGUS

COLOR CONTRAST
When the male Alpine Argus is ready to mate, he uses his gleaming colors to attract a female. Her dull colors help to hide her from predators until she has laid her eggs.

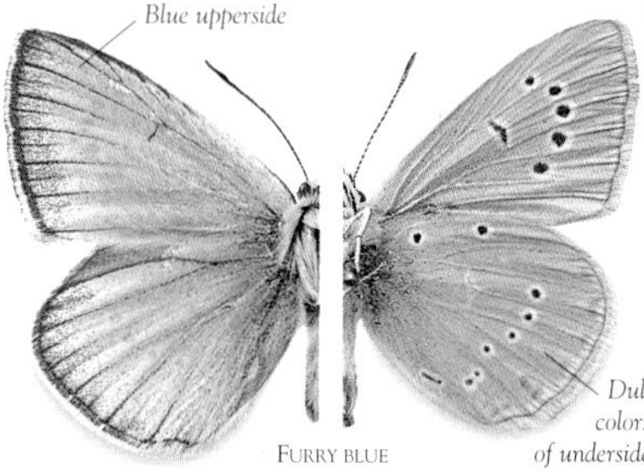

FURRY BLUE

UPPER AND UNDERSIDES
Patches of brown scent scales give this species of butterfly its furry appearance. When at rest, Blues close their wings to hide their brightly colored uppersides. The undersides are often marked with rows of tiny spots and rings on a pale background.

IDAS BLUE

The caterpillar of the Idas Blue butterfly spends the winter in the warmth and security of an ants' nest. The caterpillar secretes a sugary liquid that the ants drink. The caterpillar pupates inside the ants' nest, from which the young adult eventually emerges – crawling out into the open air to stretch its wings.

IDAS BLUE

COMMON BLUE

This butterfly is often seen flying on sunny hillsides. Its body is covered with long, hairlike scales that trap the sun's warmth and help the Common Blue survive sudden drops in temperature. It lives in both mountainous and lowland habitats in North Africa, Europe, and temperate Asia.

COMMON BLUE

IRIDESCENT COLORS

The Blues' metallic colors are roduced by the way their wing scales reflect sunshine. Their wings do not contain any blue pigment. Female Sonoran Blues have more orange on their wings han the males. They can be found mountain canyons, on cliffs, and on rocky slopes in California and northern Mexico.

SONORAN BLUE

REFERENCE SECTION

CLASSIFICATION

LIVING THINGS are classified into a series of categories according to the features that they have in common. Butterflies and moths, collectively called Lepidoptera, are a distinct group within the animal kingdom. The order Lepidoptera is divided into 120–150 families, depending on the authority consulted. These families are subdivided into over 170,000 individual species.

KINGDOM
Animalia – animal

PHYLUM
Arthropoda – animals with jointed legs

CLASS
Insecta – about one million species, arranged in 30 orders

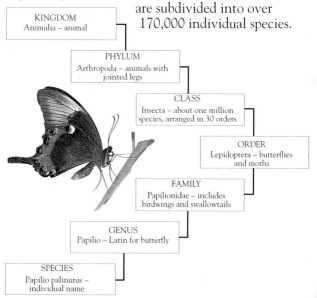

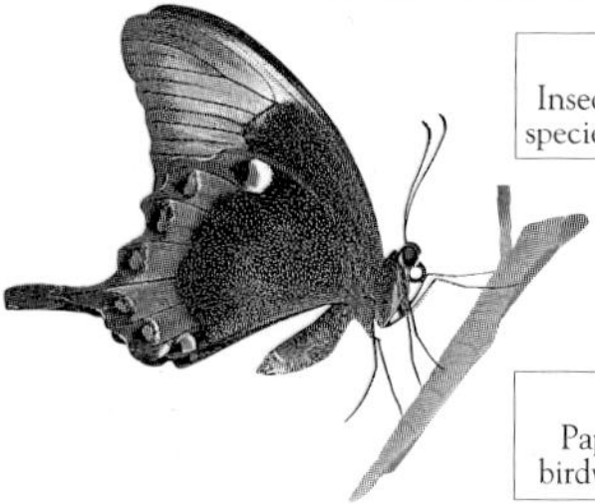

ORDER
Lepidoptera – butterflies and moths

FAMILY
Papilionidae – includes birdwings and swallowtails

GENUS
Papilio – Latin for butterfly

SPECIES
Papilio palinurus – individual name

FAMILY	EXAMPLES OF SPECIES	NOTES
ICROPTERIGIDAE	Pollen moths	Biting mouthparts in adults; mostly day fliers
ICURVARIIDAE	Long horn moths, Yucca moths	Males of some species have very long antennae; Yucca moths are essential for pollination of yucca plants
EPIALIDAE	Swift moths, Ghost moths	Wing-locking method differs from other moths; fore- and hindwings have similar shapes and vein patterns; most caterpillars bore into wood or roots
EPTICULIDAE	Leaf-mining micromoths	Caterpillars tunnel between upper and lower surface of leaves; blotchy and snake-shaped mines can be seen on leaves
NEIDAE	Clothes moths, Grain moths	Often dull-colored; feed on wool, furs, grains, and many products of economic importance
SIIDAE	Hornet moths, Clearwings	Adults are camouflaged to look like bees or wasps but they cannot sting; most are day fliers and have stem-boring caterpillars
RTRICIDAE	Apple Codling moths, Leaf-roller moths, Bell moths, Jumping Bean moths	Many species are pests of fruit, such as apples; caterpillar of Jumping Bean moth lives inside bean and causes it to "jump" when the caterpillar moves suddenly
RALIDAE	Pyralid moths	Includes a few aquatic moths; many pest species; Cactus moth used in biological control of prickly pear cactus in Australia
IYRIDIDAE	Leaf moths	The ragged outlines of many species' wings make them resemble leaves

FAMILY	EXAMPLES OF SPECIES	NOTES
ZYGAENIDAE	Burnets, Forester moths	Brightly colored; mostly day-flying; often have well-developed tongues; many have highly toxic chemicals in their bodies to deter predators
ARCTIIDAE	Tiger moths, Footmen	Caterpillars often known as "Woolly Bears"; moths are often foul-tasting and brightly colored to deter predators
GEOMETRIDAE	Geometer moths, Looper moths	Huge family of worldwide moths; some species with wingless females; many pests; caterpillars have characteristic looping movement
SPHINGIDAE	Sphinx moths	Often large and powerful fliers; some species hover to feed at flowers; large caterpillars usually have a prominent (but not dangerous) horn at the rear
COSSIDAE	Goat moths, Carpenter moths	Many do not feed in the adult stage; caterpillars are generally wood-boring and commonly called Carpenter worms
ALUCITIDAE	Many-plumed moths	Small, delicate moths; subdued colors; feathery wings; each wing divided into six lobes; small, hairy caterpillars mine flower buds
LASIOCAMPIDAE	Eggar moths, Tent caterpillar moths, Lappet moths	Adults often have very fat, hairy abdomens; tongues often reduced and nonfunctional; several pest species
SATURNIIDAE	Giant silkmoths, Emperor moths	Some of the largest moths in the world; many have well-developed eyespots; males often have feathery antennae; proboscis often reduced; adults do not fe
BOMBYCIDAE	Silkmoths	A few wild species; "cultivated" silkmot no longer exists in the wild; rounded, furry bodies; slightly hooked forewing ti caterpillar produces silk

Family	Examples of species	Notes
Lymantriidae	Tussock moths, Gypsy moths	Some species serious pests; usually hairy in appearance; dull-colored wings; lack functional tongue; do not feed as adults; females of many species cannot fly
Uraniidae	Urania moths	Small family of moths including some resembling colorful butterflies; most are tropical; many have well-developed tails on wings
Noctuidae	Owlets, Noctuids, Underwing moths	More than 20,000 species in this cosmopolitan family; caterpillars often attack roots; many are serious crop pests, including Armyworms and Cutworms
Pterophoridae	Plume moths	Small delicate moths; long-legged; narrow wings; forewings usually divided into two lobes, hindwing into three; at rest, often hold wings at right angles in "T" form
Hesperiidae	Skipper butterflies	Antennae often similar to moths; small but have large heads and stout bodies; fast-flying; caterpillars mostly feed on grass
Papilionidae	Swallowtails, Birdwing butterflies	Often have tails on hind wings; strong, gliding flight; many are tropical and brightly colored; often feed on plants poisonous to humans
Pieridae	Whites, Sulphurs, Yellow butterflies	Several pest species of whites have been accidentally spread around the world; some species are migratory
Lycaenidae	Blues, Hairstreaks, Copper butterflies	Family of over 5,000 species; often brilliant metallic blue or copper; sexes often different colors; caterpillars of many species live in association with ants
Nymphalidae	Emperors, Admirals, Fritillaries, Morpho butterflies	Over 5,000 species; forelegs reduced in size; many large and colorful species; some species migrate; commonly known as Brush-footed butterflies

Amazing Facts

THE LIFESTYLES and behavior of the 170,000 different species of butterflies and moths are almost as varied as the extraordinary colors and patterns that adorn their wings.

LIFE CYCLE

- Goat moth caterpillars take 3–4 years to fully develop.
- The life cycle of the Indian Meal moth lasts only about four weeks.
- Cold-climate species can hibernate for as long as nine months.

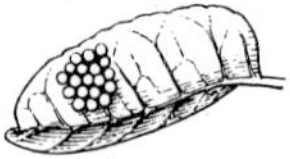

EGGS

- Aquatic moths lay their eggs under water.
- Wax moths lay their eggs in beehives.
- Danaine females lay successive batches of eggs that are fertilized by different males.

CATERPILLARS

- The caterpillar of the Hawaiian *Eupithecia* moth catches flies.
- The Puss moth caterpillar spits acid when threatened.
- The caterpillar of the Io Moth has spines that sting like a nettle.
- Larger Orange Tip caterpillars eat the smaller caterpillars.
- Birdwing caterpillars and chrysalids are eaten as delicacies in Papua New Guinea.
- The *Laetilia* caterpillar feeds on greenflies, rather than on plants.
- Large Blue caterpillars eat ant larvae.

PUPA

- The male Bagworm moth fertilizes the female while she is still in her cocoon.
- The pupa of the Striped Blue Crow is reflective and mirrors the colors around it.
- The Madagascan Moon Moth has one of the largest cocoons, which is made of shiny silver silk.
- The color of the pupa of the Great Mormon butterfly changes to suit its background.
- Gold spots on Queen butterfly pupae reflect light to distract predators.

ADULTS

• A hawkmoth from Madagascar has the longest proboscis – over 12 in (30 cm) long.

• Evening Brown butterflies usually fly at dusk and dawn.

• A migrating Monarch butterfly can fly 80 miles (130 km) per day.

• Patches of urine, full of mineral salts, attract butterflies in dry areas.

• The Zebra butterfly emits a foul smell to ward off predators.

• Male Long horn moths have antennae up to six times the length of their bodies.

• Sphinx moths have sharp protective spines on their legs.

• In Japan, butterflies symbolize the souls of the dead.

• Vampire or Calpe moths from Southeast Asia can puncture skin and suck blood.

SHAPE AND SIZE

• Many-plumed moths have wings divided into six segments.

• Tails on the hind wings distract predators.

• The wing tips of the giant Atlas moth look like snakes' heads.

• Ctenuchid moths resemble the shape of inedible Lycid beetles.

• The female Queen Alexandra's Birdwing is the largest butterfly – it has a 6–11 in (15–28 cm) wingspan.

• The *Thysania agrippina* moth has the largest wingspan: 9–12 in (23–30 cm).

• One of the smallest butterlies is the Grass Jewel with a ⅓ in–⅔-in (1–1.5-cm) wingspan.

• Nepticulid moths are the smallest moths – ⅛ in (0.3 cm) wingspan.

• The Hercules moth is the largest moth in the world.

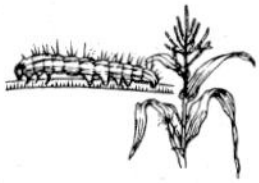

PESTS

• Armyworm caterpillars may destroy hundreds of hectares of crops.

• The *Filodes* moth feeds on moisture around the eyes of cattle and can spread diseases.

• In its lifetime, a single Black Arches moth caterpillar can eat about 1,000 pine needles and damage as many again.

• Wax moth caterpillars feed on beeswax and badly damage beehives.

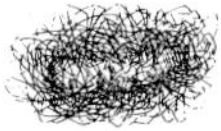

FRIENDS

• 40,000 Silkmoth cocoons could provide enough silk to encircle the earth at the Equator with a single thread.

• In Australia, the voracious Cactus Moth has helped farmers to clear large areas of land of prickly pear cacti.

HABITATS UNDER THREAT

BEFORE HUMAN LIFE flourished on Earth, habitats and animal and plant species were destroyed purely by climatic changes or natural disasters such as volcanic eruptions. However, people have increased the pressures on the natural world, causing pollution and using land for agriculture, timber, mining, and building projects. Moths and butterflies living in affected habitats are among the first species to suffer.

HABITAT	THREATS	SPECIES AT RISK
Rain forests 	Rain forests, which are particularly rich in Lepidoptera, are under threat from logging for timber, clearing for farmland, and mining.	The Esmeralda, Brazilian Dynastor, Blue Morpho, Australian Atlas moth, Queen Alexandra's Birdwing
Tropical dry forests 	Less common than rain forests, tropical dry forests are threatened by fires and clearance for farming. Countries such as Costa Rica have made efforts to preserve these special habitats.	Tiger Pierid, Leaf Moth, Macrogonia Moth
Temperate forests 	Many areas have been cleared for agriculture or replaced by coniferous forests. Some areas have been affected by acid rain and by polluted water drained off from nearby farmland. A rich source of timber for industry and furniture.	Purple Emperor, Silver-washed Fritillary, Pearly Eye, Black Hairstreak

HABITAT	THREATS	SPECIES AT RISK
Mountains 	Overgrazing on the lower slopes and increased use of the higher slopes for skiing and other winter vacation resorts put many mountain habitats at risk.	Apollo, Checkerspot, Alpine Erebia, Gavarnie Blue, Mountain Small White, Corsican Swallowtail, Long-tailed Beauty moth
Wetlands 	There are few places in the world where wetlands are not under some threat. Drainage usually provides fertile farmland or land may be used for forestry. In some areas, peat extraction on a commercial scale is a serious threat.	Marsh Fritillary, Bog Copper, Large Copper, Mitchell's Satyr, Bog Fritillary, Mulberry Wing butterfly, False Ringlet
Pastures 	Traditional pastures are often enriched with fertilizers to enhance feed available for grazing livestock. Aggressive species of plants take over and this reduces the diversity of other plants and, in turn, the variety of *Lepidoptera*.	Small Blue, Scarce Copper, Tessellated Skipper, Beardgrass Skipper, Eltham Copper
Grasslands 	Grasslands are now often seeded with "improved" types of grass, which make better animal feed but support fewer species of butterfly. Grasslands are also under intense pressure for housing and other building development.	Southern Skipperling, Large Blue, Twin-spot Fritillary, Meadow Fritillary
Nature reserves 	In order to maintain balance, nature reserves must be managed. Long and short grasses support different species of butterflies and moths. By removing "undesirable" invasive plants, the species that feed on them also disappear.	Species affected depend on management plan; what may be good for one species may be bad for another

OBSERVING

BUTTERFLIES AND MOTHS can be disturbed by the slightest movement, so you will need plenty of patience to get near enough to study them. Probably the best time to observe them is when they are eating and drinking. In time, you will soon discover the best sites.

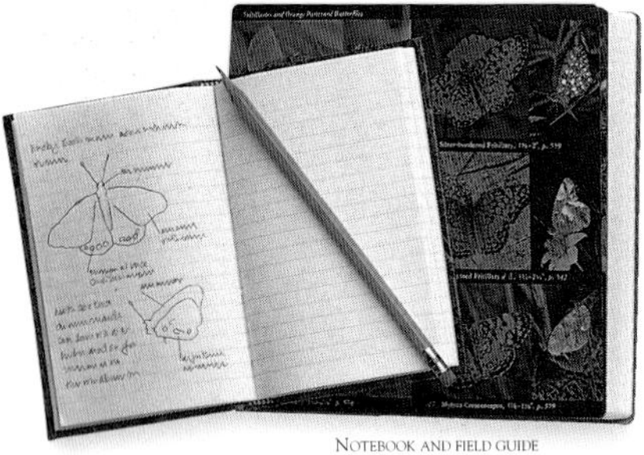
NOTEBOOK AND FIELD GUIDE

WATCHING CODE

- Do not kill species in order to identify them.
- Examine them in a glass tube or pill box; release them unharmed.
- Some countries do not allow collecting or the use of nets.
- Certain species are legally protected.
- Take care not to damage the habitat or trample on crops.

YOU WILL NEED

CAMERA

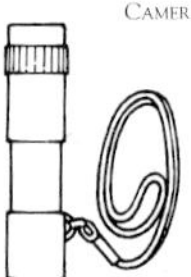
SHORT-FOCUS TELESCOPE

PILL BOXES

RECORDING YOUR OBSERVATIONS

Keep a notebook to make quick sketches and record observations on where and when the insect was found, its behavior, appearance, and habitat. A short-focus telescope will reveal details barely visible to the naked eye and a field guide will help you check your identification of the species. Take a camera along; photographs are useful for further study.

Where to look

Egg-laying sites
These sites need to be protected; look on the hidden undersides of leaves and near buds.

Caterpillar food plants
Look for caterpillars feeding on leaves and blades of grass. Many larvae are camouflaged.

Sheltered spots
Butterflies bask in the sun, sheltered from wind. Many species lay their eggs in sheltered spots.

Feeding stations
Flowers are the best food supply; butterflies and moths are attracted by their color and scent.

Hedgerows
Many butterflies and moths can be found on plants, sheltered underneath shrubs.

Damp ground
In hot climates, moths and butterflies drink from the damp ground in forests.

Liquid sources
Butterflies and moths can be found feeding on juicy, overripe fruit or drinking from puddles.

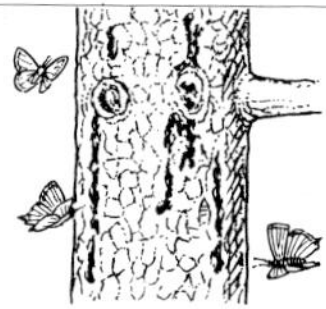

Oozing sap
Moths and butterflies gorge on sap oozing from trees. At night, use a flashlight to see moths.

Light
Moths fly toward light at night; look for them on store windows and streetlights.

REARING

ONE OF THE BEST ways to study moths and butterflies is to rear them from eggs. Many species can be bred in captivity. Remember to find out which plants the caterpillars eat before the eggs hatch.

CHOSEN SPECIES
It takes a couple of months to rear Peacock butterfly from egg to adul

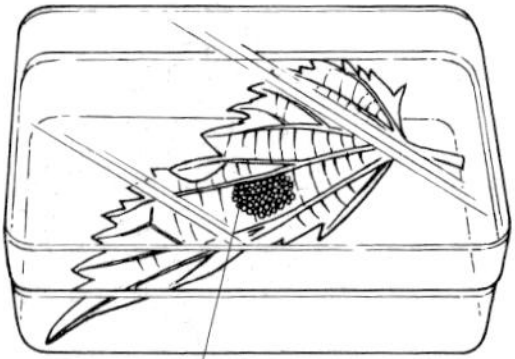

1 Place eggs laid by a captive female (or eggs found on nettles in the field) in a small plastic box. Keep the box closed to ensure that the leaves do not dry out. When they hatch, transfer the small caterpillars to a larger container.

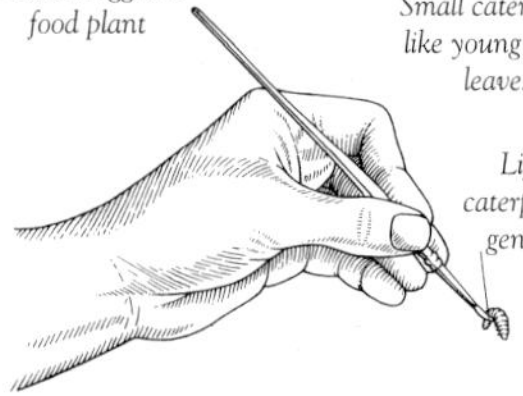

2 Handle the caterpillars as little as possible. Use a fine paintbrush to transfer a caterpillar from one container to another.

3 Place leaves of the caterpillars' food plant in a clear plastic container. To absorb excess moisture, place absorbent paper in the bottom or replace the container's lid with gauze. Feed the caterpillars regularly with fresh leaves.

4 Transfer the caterpillars to a larger container as they grow larger. Put fresh cuttings from the caterpillars' food plant in a cage made of netting, or inside a clear plastic container with a perforated lid to provide adequate light and ventilation. The food must be inspected regularly and replaced when necessary.

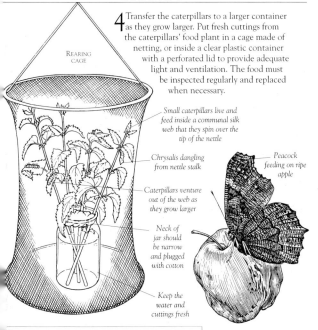

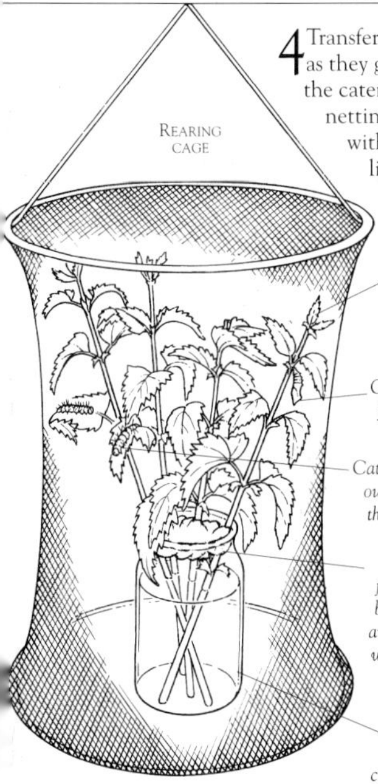
REARING CAGE
Small caterpillars live and feed inside a communal silk web that they spin over the tip of the nettle
Chrysalis dangling from nettle stalk
Caterpillars venture out of the web as they grow larger
Neck of jar should be narrow and plugged with cotton
Keep the water and cuttings fresh

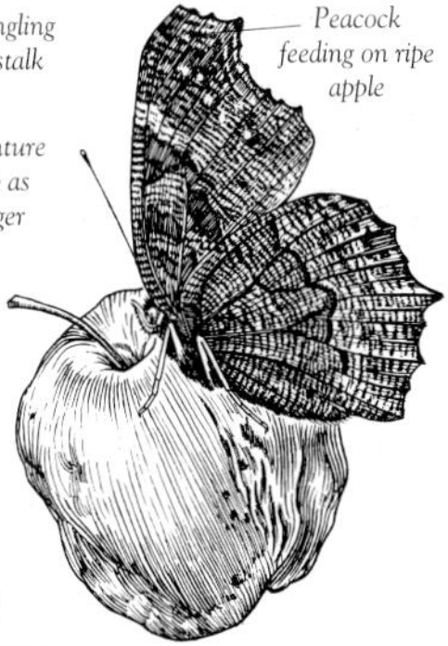
Peacock feeding on ripe apple

WARNING BOX

- It is illegal to release ıon-native species into he wild.
- Releasing captive pecies can upset mating ›atterns among the local vild population.
- Consult a conservation group before releasing captive-bred species.
- If large numbers are released, you could create competition if food is scarce.

5 Keep the adult female butterfly for a short period to obtain eggs. Feed her on a weak sugar solution, cut flowers, or very ripe fruit. Release the butterfly if it is a species native to your country.

BUTTERFLY GARDEN

NECTAR-BEARING PLANTS attract moths and butterflies to gardens all over the world. To provide a continuous food supply, grow a range of plants that bloom at different times of the year. If you grow plants that the caterpillars can eat, the insects may breed in your garden.

BLUE TRIANGLE
This colorful butterfly is frequently seen in Australian gardens and is widespread throughout Asia. It feeds on many garden plants, such as buddleia, hebe, lantana, and verbena.

SUMMER BUTTERFLIES
Throughout Europe, Asia, the US, Canada, and Hawaii, the Red Admiral is quite common on all garden plants, especially after a long, warm summer. The caterpillars often feed on nettles in semishaded areas.

SILVER-STRIPED HAWKMOTH

nk base to hind wing

NECTAR

Hawkmoths use their long proboscis to suck nectar from the deep tubular florets of honeysuckle. Hovering over flowers, Silver-Striped Hawkmoths visit gardens across Europe, Africa, and Australasia.

Night-scented flowers, such as honeysuckle, attract moths

ouded Yellow utterflies feed on clovers, ch in nectar

WILD GARDEN

If you leave a small part of the garden to grow wild, you will attract a wider variety of species. Many females lay their eggs on wild grasses and nettles, the food plants of many caterpillars.

LAVENDER

loths and utterflies e strongly scented flowers

MONARCH

Large wings

GARDEN VISITORS

As Monarchs migrate across North America, they visit garden flowers to "fuel up" for their journey and the winter. Less frequently, they can be spotted in gardens in Europe and Australasia. Monarchs have been recorded feeding on more than 24 varieties of milkweed plants.

Resources

These are just some of the centers around the world where you can obtain further information about moths and butterflies.

COLLECTIONS

AUSTRALIA

Australian National Insect Collection
Care of CSIRO Division of Entomology
P.O. Box 1700
Canberra, ACT 2601

BRAZIL

Wildlife Museum
Quinta da Boa Vista
Avenida Dom Pedro II
São Cristóvão
Rio de Janeiro

CANADA

National Museum of Natural Sciences
Metcalfe & McLeod Sts.
Ottowa, Ontario

FRANCE

Musée National d'Histoire Naturelle
Jardin des Plantes
Rue Cuvier, Paris 75005

GERMANY

Museum für Naturkunde der Humboldt-Universität zu Berlin
Invalidenstrasse 43
D-10115 Berlin

JAPAN

Osaka Museum of Natural History
Higashisumiyoshi-ku
Osaka

MALAYSIA

National Museum of Malaysia
Damansara
Kuala Lumur

SOUTH AFRICA

South African Museum
P.O. Box 61
Cape Town 8000

SPAIN

Museo Nacional de Ciencias Naturales
José Gutiérrez Abascal
28006 Madrid

SWEDEN

Swedish Museum of Natural History
P.O. Box 50007
S-104 05 Stockholm

UNITED KINGDOM

Natural History Museum
Cromwell Road
London SW7 5BD

UNITED STATES

There are many; here are six of the largest in the US:

Allyn Museum of Entomology
3621 Bay Shore Rd.
Sarasota, FL 34234

American Museum of Natural History
Central Park West
at 79th St.
New York, NY 10024

Bishop Museum
1525 Bernice Street
Honolulu, HI 96817

Carnegie Museum of Natural History
4400 Forbes Ave.
Pittsburgh, PA 15213

Denver Museum of Natural History
2001 Colorado Blvd.
Denver, CO 80205

National Museum of Natural History
Smithsonian Institution
Washington, DC 20560

CONSERVATION SOCIETIES

Specializing in insect conservation:

UNITED KINGDOM

The Butterfly Conservation Society
Manor Yard
East Lulworth
Wareham
Dorset, BH20 5QP

World Wildlife Fund
Panda House
Weyside Park
Godalming, Surrey
GU7 1XR

UNITED STATES

National Audubon Society
700 Broadway
New York, NY 10003

The Xerces Society
4828 SE Hawthorne Blvd.
Portland, OR 97215

BUTTERFLY GARDENS

There are many local butterfly farms – larger wildlife organizations can give more information:

UNITED KINGDOM

London Zoo
Regents Park
London NW1 4RY

Worldlife and Lullington Silk Farm
Crompton House
Nr. Sherbourne
Dorset DT9 4QN

UNITED STATES

There are over 100 in the US; these are two of the best-known

Butterfly World
Tradewinds Park
3600 West Sample Rd.
Coconut Creek, FL 33073

The Day Butterfly Center
Callaway Gardens
PO Box 2000
Pine Mountain,
GA 31822

INSECT SOCIETIES

INTERNATIONAL

Largest and best-known international organization for amateurs and professionals interested in the study of Lepidoptera:

The Lepidopterists' Society
c/o Julian P. Donahue,
Assistant Secretary
Natural History Museum
of Los Angeles County
900 Exposition Blvd.
Los Angeles, CA 90007

BOOKS AND EQUIPMENT

Best supply source for entomological books and equipment in the US

Bioquip Products
17803 LaSalle Ave.
Gardena, CA 90248

Glossary

ABDOMEN
Segmented rear part of the body behind the thorax. It contains the digestive and reproductive organs.

ANDROCONIA
Special scent scales, found in male butterflies, that disperse pheromones. See PHEROMONES.

ANTENNAE
Sensory organs on the heads of adults and caterpillars. They are mainly used for smelling and touching.

BROADLEAF
Having wide leaves (deciduous trees).

CAMOUFLAGE
To disguise the body with colors, markings, or patterns that blend with the surroundings.

CHRYSALIS
Butterfly pupa. See PUPA.

CLASPERS
Two pincers on the end of the abdomen; the male uses them to grasp the female while mating.

COCOON
A protective silk case, which some caterpillars weave around their bodies before pupating.

COLONY
A community of individuals of the same species that live together.

COMPOUND EYE
An eye consisting of many light-sensitive units called ommatidia.

DIGESTION
The process by which food is broken down and absorbed into the body.

ECDYSIS
The molting process by which the caterpillar changes its skin as it grows larger.

ESTIVATE
To remain dormant during heat or drought in order to survive.

EXOSKELETON
The hard, external covering of the body.

EYESPOTS
Circular markings on the wings that look like eyes to deter predators.

FERTILIZATION
The union of a male sex cell and a female sex cell during the reproduction process.

HIBERNATION
The resting state in which butterflies and moths pass the winter in temperate regions. All the body processes slow down to conserve energy.

HONEYDEW
A sweet, sticky liquid excreted by aphids, which comes from the sap of the plants on which they feed.

IRIDESCENT
Bright rainbowlike coloring that shimmers and changes constantly.

LARVA
The wingless, immature form, which is also known as a caterpillar.

LEPIDOPTERA
The order of insects to which butterflies and moths belong.

MANDIBLE
One of a pair of jawlike mouthparts used to bite or chew food.

METAMORPHOSIS
The series of changes in body structure that occurs during the life cycle of moths and butterflies. Moths

nd butterflies undergo omplete metamorphosis, hich comprises four stinct phases – egg, terpillar, pupa, and lult stage.

IGRATION
ight to a new area, ten prompted by asonal or climatic ange or the need for esh food supplies.

IMICRY
ne process whereby e species of butterfly moth copies the pearance and behavior another species to gain otection from edators.

ECTAR
sugary fluid produced plants that courages butterflies d moths to visit and llinate flowers.

OCTURNAL
be active at night and rest during the day.

ELLI
nple eyes that pond mainly to light d shade.

IMATIDIUM
single facet of a npound eye.

ERWINTER
e HIBERNATION.

PALPS
Taste organs beside the mouthparts on the head.

PHEROMONES
Scented chemical substances released by butterflies and moths of both sexes to signal that they are ready to mate.

PIGMENT
A colored substance that occurs in plant and animal tissues.

POLLEN
A dustlike powder in flowers that contains the male sex cells.

POLLINATION
The transfer of pollen from the male parts to the female parts of flowers or cones so that seeds can develop.

PROBOSCIS
Elongated mouthparts that usually act as a feeding tube.

PROLEGS
Suckerlike structures along the caterpillar's abdomen that lack joints but function as legs.

PUPA, PUPAL STAGE
The inactive, nonfeeding stage in the life cycle during which the caterpillar is transformed into an adult.

SCALES
Flattened, platelike hairs that cover moths and butterflies.

SPECIES
A group of animals or plants that can breed only with each other to produce fertile offspring.

SPINNERET
Organ in caterpillars through which silk, secreted by the silk gland, is spun into threads and pushed out into the air to form webs and cocoons.

SPIRACLES
External openings of the breathing tubes, located on the sides of the body.

THORAX
Middle part of the body, between the head and the abdomen.

ULTRAVIOLET
Light beyond the violet end of the color spectrum, invisible to the human eye but visible to insects.

WARNING COLORS
Bold, conspicuous colors to warn predators that a butterfly or moth is poisonous.

WINGSPAN
Measurement from one wing tip to the other.

Common and scientific names

Adonis Blue
Lysandra bellargus
African Grass Blue
Zizeeria knysna
African Leaf Butterfly
Kallimoides rumia
African Moon Moth
Argema mimosae
African Ringlet
Ypthima asterope
Alpine Argus
Albulina orbitulus
Alpine Skipper
Oreisplanus munionga
Antler Moth
Cerapteryx graminis
Arctic Fritillary
Clossiana chariclea
Atlas moth
Attacus atlas

Banksia Moth
Danima banksiae
Bent-wing Ghost moth
Zelotypia stacyi
Bhutan Glory
Bhutanitis lidderdalei
Bicolor Commodore
Limenitis zayla
Black-and-white Tiger
Danaus affinis
Black Arches
Lymantria monacha
Black-veined White
Aporia crataegi
Blue Pansy
Junonia orithya
Blue Tharops
Menander menander
Blue Triangle
Graphium sarpedon
Bogong Moth
Agrotis infusa
Brazilian Morpho
Morpho aega
Brazilian Skipper
Calpodes ethlius
Brimstone Moth
Opisthograptis luteolata
Brindled Beauty
Lycia hirtaria
Brown China-mark
Elophila nympheata
Brown Hooded Owlet
Cucullia convexipennis
Buckeye
Junonia coenia
Butler's Brahmin
Dactylocerus swanzii

Cairns Birdwing
Ornithoptera priamus
California Dog-face
Zerene eurydice
Cardinal Fritillary
Pandoriana pandora
Cinnabar Moth
Tyria jacobeae
Citrus Swallowtail
Papilio demodocus
Cleopatra
Gonepteryx cleopatra
Clouded Yellow
Colias croceus
Cloudless Giant Sulphur
Phoebis sennae
Comma
Polygonia c-album
Common Blue
Polyommatus icarus
Common Brown
Heteronympha merope
Common Clothes Moth
Tineola bisselliella
Common Eggfly
Hypolimnas bolina
Common Emperor
Bunaea alcinoe
Common Glider
Neptis sappho
Common Imperial Blue
Jalmenus evagoras
Common Mormon
Papilio polytes
Common Opal
Poecilmitis thysbe
Cramer's Blue Morpho
Morpho rhetenor
Crimson Speckled Moth
Utetheisa pulchella
Crimson Tip
Colotis danae
Cruiser Butterfly
Vindula erota

ynthia's Fritillary
Euphydryas cynthia

ark Chopper
Gonometa postica
ark Green Fritillary
Argynnis aglaja
eath's Head
lawkmoth
Acherontia atropos
ingy Skipper
Erynnis tages
iva Moth
Divana diva
oherty's Longtail
Himantopterus dohertyi
otted Checkerspot
Poladryas minuta
rinker Moth
Philudoria potatoria
ryad Butterfly
Minois dryas
uke of Burgundy
Hamearis lucina

astern Flat Skipper
Netrocoryne repanda
lephant Hawkmoth
Deilephila elpenor
mperor Gum Moth
Opodiphthera eucalypti
smeralda Butterfly
Cithaerias esmeralda
vening Brown
Melanitis leda

alse Clothes Moth
Hofmannophila pseudospretella
Fiery Campylotes
Campylotes desgodinsi
Forester
Adscita statices
Foxy Charaxes
Charaxes jasius
Freak Butterfly
Calinaga buddha
Furry Blue
Agrodiaetus dolus

Garden Tiger
Arctia caja
Ghost Moth
Hepialus humuli
Giant African Skipper
Pyrrhochalcia iphis
Giant Agrippa
Thysania agrippina
Giant Anthelid
Chelepteryx collesi
Glasswing
Acraea andromacha
Goat Moth
Cossus cossus
Golden Clearwing
Albuna oberthuri
Grass Jewel
Freyeria trochylus
Great Oak Beauty
Boarmia roboraria
Great Orange Tip
Hebomoia glaucippe
Grizzled Skipper
Pyrgus malvae
Guineafowl Butterfly
Hamanumidia daedalus
Gypsy Moth
Lymantria dispar

Harvester
Feniseca tarquinius
Heath Fritillary
Mellicta athalia
Herald
Scoliopteryx libatrix
Hercules Moth
Coscinocera hercules
Hermit
Chazara briseis
Hewitson's Blue
Hairstreak
Thecla coronata
High Mountain Blue
Agriades franklinii
Holly Blue
Celastrina argiolus
Hornet Moth
Sesia apiformis
Hummingbird
Hawkmoth
Macroglossum stellatarum

Idas Blue
Lycaeides idas
Indian Leaf Butterfly
Kallima inachus
Indian Moon Moth
Actias selene
Io Moth
Automeris io

Japanese Swallowtail
Papilio xuthus

Large Blue
Maculinea arion
Large Blue Charaxes
Charaxes bohemani
Large Checkered Skipper
Heteropterus morpheus
Large Copper
Lycaena dispar
Large Heath
Coenonympha tullia
Large Skipper
Ochlodes venatas
Large Tortoiseshell
Nymphalis polychloros
Large Tree Nymph
Idea leuconoe
Large White
Pieris brassicae
Leopard Moth
Zeuzera pyrina
Little Tiger Blue
Tarucus balkanicus
Lobster Moth
Stauropus fagi
Long-tailed Skipper
Urbanus proteus

Madagascan Moon moth
Argema mittrei
Madagascan Sunset moth
Chrysiridia riphearia
Magpie Moth
Abraxas grossulariata
Malay Lacewing
Cethosia hypsaea
Many-plumed Moth
Orneodes dohertyi
Marbled White
Melanargia galathea
Marsh Fritillary
Eurodryas aurinia
Meadow Brown
Maniola jurtina
Monarch
Danaus plexippus
Moorland Clouded
Yellow
Colias palaeno
Morgan's sphinx
Xanthopan morganii
Mother-of-pearl Morpho
Morpho laertes
Mourning Cloak
Nymphalis antiopa

Northern Clouded Yellow
Colias hecla

Oak Silkmoth
Antheraea harti
Old Lady Moth
Mormo maura
Oleander Hawkmoth
Daphnis nerii
Orange Albatross
Appias nero
Orange Sulphur
Colias eurytheme
Orange Tip
Anthocharis cardamines
Orizaba Silkmoth
Rothschildia orizaba
Owl Butterfly
Caligo idomeneus
Owl Moth
Brahmaea wallichii

Painted Lady
Cynthia cardui
Palla Butterfly
Palla ussheri
Palm Skipper
Zophopetes dysmephila
Passion-vine Butterfly
Heliconius ismenius
Peacock
Inachis io
Peak White Butterfly
Pontia callidice
Peppered Moth
Biston betularia
Piedmont Ringlet
Erebia meolans
Pine Emperor Moth
Nudaurelia cytherea
Pine Processionary
Thaumetopoea pityocampa
Pine-tree Lappet
Dendrolimus pini
Pine White
Neophasia menapia
Pink-barred Sallow
Xanthia togata
Pirate Butterfly
Catacroptera cloanthe
Poplar Hawkmoth
Laothoe populi
Postman Butterfly
Heliconius melpomene
Purple-edged Copper
Palaeochrysophanus hippothoe
Purple Hairstreak
Quercusia quercus
Puss Moth
Cerura vinula

Queen Alexandra's Birdwing
Ornithoptera alexandrae

Queen Butterfly
Danaus gilippus

Queen Cracker
Hamadryas arethusa

Rajah Brooke's Birdwing
Ornithoptera brookiana

Red Underwing
Catocala nupta

Regent Skipper
Euschemon rafflesia

Ringlet
Aphantopus hyperantus

Robin Moth
Hyalophora cecropia

Royal Walnut Moth
Citheronia regalis

Ruby Tiger
Phragmatobia fuliginosa

Scarlet Tiger
Callimorpha dominula

Schulze's Agrias
Agrias claudia

Silkmoth
Bombyx mori

Silver Butterfly
Argyrophorus argenteus

Silver Hairstreak
Chrysozephyrus syla

Silver-spotted Skipper
Hesperia comma

Silver-striped Hawkmoth
Hippotion celerio

Silver-studded Blue
Plebejus argus

Silver-washed Fritillary
Argynnis paphia

Small Copper
Lycaena phlaeas

Smaller Wood Nymph
Ideopsis gaura

Small Postman
Heliconius erato

Small Tortoiseshell
Aglais urticae

Small White
Pieris rapae

Sonoran Blue
Philotes sonorensis

Spanish Festoon
Zerynthia rumina

Spanish Moon Moth
Graellsia isabellae

Speckled Wood
Pararge aegeria

Splendid Ghost Moth
Aenetus mirabilis

Striped Blue Crow
Euploea mulciber

Striped Hawkmoth
Hyles lineata

Swallowtail
Papilio machaon

Swamp Metalmark
Calephelis mutica

Tawny Rajah
Charaxes bernardus

Tiger Pierid
Dismorphia amphione

Tiger Swallowtail
Papilio glaucus

Two-tailed Pasha
Charaxes jasius

Vampire Moth
Calyptra eustrigata

Variable Burnet Moth
Zygaena ephialtes

Verdant Sphinx
Euchloron megaera

Viceroy
Basilarchia archippus

Wall Brown
Lasiommata megera

Water Tiger
Paracles laboulbeni

White Admiral
Ladoga camilla

White Ermine
Spilosoma lubricipeda

White Peacock
Anartia jatrophae

Woodland Grayling
Hipparchia fagi

Wood White
Leptidea sinapis

Yellow Coster
Acraea vesta

Yellow-spot Blue
Candalides xanthospilos

Zebra Butterfly
Colobura dirce

Zebra Swallowtail
Eurytides marcellus

Index

Acknowledgments

Dorling Kindersley would like to thank:
Hilary Bird for the index; Densey Clyne for advice on Australian species; Sandy Atkins and Gwilym Lewis at Kew Gardens, Dr Legg at the Booth Museum, and Dr Ackery at the Natural History Museum who all provided information; Alistair Dougall for invaluable editorial assistance.

Photographs by:
Peter Anderson, Geoff Brightling, Jane Burton, Peter Chadwick, Geoff Dann, Neil Fletcher, Frank Greenaway (Natural History Museum), Jacqui Hurst, Colin Keates (Natural History Museum), Dave King, Oxford Scientific Films, Andrew McRobb, Kim Taylor, Matthew Ward, Jerry Young (15tr, 21tl, 30tl, 32-33b, 39cb, 41br, 42c).

Illustrations by:
Peter Bailey, Julia Cobbold, Nick Hall, Brian Hargreaves, Nick Hewetson, Mark Iley, John Still, Tommy Swahn, Gill Tomblin, Peter Visscher, John Woodcock.

Picture credits:
t top; *b* bottom; *c* center; *l* left; *r* right
The publishers would like to thank the following for their permission to reproduce their photographs:

Booth Museum, Brighton 23b; Bruce Coleman Ltd/Dr Eckart Pott 44cl; /Hans Reinhard 80-81; /Leonard Lee Rue 51br, 90-91; /Kevin Rushby 25cl; /John Shaw 51t, 116-117; Michael & Patricia Fogden 29br; Ecoscene/W. Lawler 48b; Forest Light/Alan Watson 50cl, 52-53; The Natural History Museum, London 12tl, 19b, 20c, 27cl, 43cl, 43br, 44br, 45tc, 45c, 48tr, 48b, 65b, 77t, 83c, 84b, 85t, 85b, 86cr, 87t, 103tr, 104b, 107b, 111c, 115, 119cl, 123t, 123c, 124b, 129tr, 144cr, 145br; Natural Science Photos/Nigel Charles 121t; Nature Photographers Ltd 123bl; /Jean Hall 47tr; Microscopix/Andrew Syred 130-131; Oxford Scientific Films /Michael Fogden 10-11; /Muzz Murray 46b; Premaphotos Wildlife/K.G Preston-Mafham 50br, 51cr, 66-67, 108-109.

Special thanks to the Natural History Museum, London, where most of the specimens that appear in this book were photographed.

Every effort has been made to trace the copyright holders, and we apologize in advance for any unintentional omissions. We would be pleased to insert the appropriate acknowledgment in any subsequent edition of this publication.